YASUMI – THE RISING SUN HAS SET

A catalogue record of this book is available from the British Library

First Edition: November 2005

ISBN: 1-84375-190-9

To order additional copies of this book please visit:
http://www.upso.co.uk/brendabarks

Published by: UPSO Ltd
5 Stirling Road, Castleham Business Park,
St Leonards-on-Sea, East Sussex TN38 9NW United Kingdom
Tel: 01424 853349 Fax: 0870 191 3991
Email: info@upso.co.uk Web: http://www.upso.co.uk

A true story of a young soldier

YASUMI – THE RISING SUN HAS SET

by

Brenda Barks

UPSO

Dedication

In loving memory of my dad. To Joan - my mum - who in 2001 handed me dad's wartime correspondence, diary, photos and medals.

Having decided to type the diary, as most pages were becoming fragile and the ink beginning to fade, I realised that this was my first ever sighting of the diary, as dad – like so many other Japanese PoWs - would never talk about those World War 2 years, but here for you, are first-hand historic accounts, penned by William George Holt of the Royal Artillery, Field Regiment, and published thanks to the encouragement of family and friends.

The story you are about to read is a true story, from being a young soldier in 1939 to becoming a Japanese PoW. The diary was confiscated in December 1943.

Chapter One

25 September 1939
ON LEAVING CHEAM

The dawn is hardly breaking as we march off "in column of route" down The Avenue bound for the Station. 700 pairs of heavy army boots moving up and down along the asphalte road disturbing Cheam in it's early morning slumbers, will serve as a last noisy memory that the 92nd Field Regiment Royal Artillery has left the comfort of civvy billets for the barns and haylofts of France.

As we swing past N° 48, I transfer my kitbag to my left shoulder so that I can pass a last wave to Winnie, who stands snivelling at the door. Poor Winnie, she worked long hours as a maid but, when we four – Joe, Jack, Len and myself were billeted in the house, she worked even longer and harder. For 3 weeks she had mothered us, waking us every morning with a cup of tea and preparing us a super breakfast before she packed us off for morning parade. The first morning we used the front door. When she saw what a mess that four pairs of Army boots could make of a polished hall floor, she hastily decided that we must use the back door.

This was hardly to the gardener's advantage for the back door at the bottom of the garden was half sheltered by an apple tree in fruit, and all four of us strongly believed that "An apple a day keeps the doctor away" – as long as Lewis the gardener, doesn't see you taking them.

We are half way down The Avenue now. There was the field we used as a gun park. We spent a busy fortnight in there when the new 25 pounder guns came to replace our 18 pounders, and the Guy Tractors came, still in their factory painted grey coating. We worked against time to put on their war time camouflage paint. There was the battery parade ground where I first saw the 80 Army reservists, sent to us to replace the men too young to go abroad. We Territorials, were only "Saturday night soldiers" and had been told we might learn a thing or two from these "old soldiers" shortly to be sprinkled in our midst.

We did. We learnt that these "old soldiers" had served their time with the Coastal 9.2s, with the mountain pack mule artillery in India, and with the fortress guns of Spike Island - but they had never seen the 25 pounder field gun before in their lives !

The "drivers" the War Office had sent us for our tractors never knew anything about a footbrake and clutch because in their time they had been horse drivers.

However, we soon taught them the "new fangled ideas" in the mechanised army of today and they gradually caught on the idea.

We turn left at the railway bridge and shorten our steps down the steep decline to the station gates. At the gate is the bus stop, where last night I wished Mum, Lilly and Rose a last Goodbye before they got on the bus for home.

We have only been mobilised 3 weeks and are already bound for France without any Embarkation Leave. When Mrs Kneen knew we were shortly leaving, she very kindly invited my people, Joe's, Jack's and Len's people down to a Sunday night tea as a Farewell Party. Goodbyes are always painful but have to be endured. It was certainly a golden opportunity of having a last pleasant evening with my family before sailing for France.

I hope I convinced Mum, as we were waiting for their bus home late last night that I really was looking forward to going overseas as a great adventure, and that she had no need to worry. I know I almost convinced myself.

We clatter onto the station platform and dump our kit. When I first joined the Artillery, my only equipment consisted of a haversack, water bottle and kitbag. On the outbreak of War, our equipment was called in and we got the new mechanised Army pattern equipment.

Instead of a small kit, we now carry side haversack, web harness, water bottle, back pack, gas cape, respirator, tin hat, greatcoat and kitbag.

"Join the Artillery" Dad advised me, "...avoid the Infantry – they carry too much". But now in this equipment, I look like a bonny Christmas tree.

Chapter Two

27 September 1939
ON FINDING MYSELF ABROAD - FRANCE

When I had picked the last two weeks of September at work, for my annual holiday, I did not expect for one moment that I would ever get it. War clouds had hung over the world for a year and things were rapidly moving to a climax. Nearly everybody at the 'Ocean' was enrolled in some wartime organisation ready for the showdown inevitably coming. In the City Branch, 28 out of 32 were in something, TA, ARP or AFS.

For the past 18 weeks we had been busy working overtime, duplicating files and reinforcing the basements against bombs yet to fall. Charlie Scobie, and other Naval reservists, had never returned to work since they went for their annual fortnights training with the Fleet last July. They were already mobilised. Ever since the middle of August we had been becoming less and less in number as Home Defence and Ack Ack units mobilised. I never expected I would be called out yet – for the TA Field Army would only be called when the balloon went up.

Then Friday 1st September. Many had not turned up at work that morning. Every other telephone call sent somebody scrambling for his hat and coat and with a few hurried "Goodbye" and Good Luck" from the others, he would hurry off to his unit to become Sgt Blank or Private X. "Happy" had just brought in the latest scare news "Germany invades Poland : Warsaw Bombed".

Before I could realise the full significance of this, Charlie Giles came blustering in and blurted out that I was wanted on the phone. Hell – I had been expecting it long enough but now it had come, my heart was in my throat. "Hello – is that you Will?" Mum did not recognise my voice – nor I hers. "A form has come. Its marked "URGENT – MOBILISATION".

I ran home – a bus would take too long! Dad had my kit and equipment laid out and Mum had a day's rations made up for me. Young Tom was home. He has been in the ARP since he was 14 years old and at 15 is qualified in Gas and Warden's duties.

I didn't want Mum to see me off but Dad came up to the depot. We had a drink before we went in, buses fully laden with troops were already pulling away. London was being cleared of troops at once, in case of bombing. On the way to Kennington we had called in at the Rollco to say goodbye to Rose and Lilly. Lilly had started crying. I hardly felt much better but things like that mustn't be shown. "Don't be silly, it will all blow over in 3 weeks" – I said. But 3 weeks later, I am kicking the cobbled roads of Cherbourg. The taxis here have a ridiculous high pitched horn. The French reservists look conspicuous in sky blue uniforms and the policemen, matelots, and road-sweepers all wear uniforms like we use on a comic stage.

October 1939 : ST REMY DU PLEIN
In this comic country you can have a pocketful of small change and be almost broke.

The "Advance Party" of guns, tractors and lorries, left England from Bristol 3 days before we left Southampton. Being the Advance Party we expected them to be waiting for us in France. Actually we have waited 3 weeks instead before they arrived. Torpedo scares, real and otherwise, gave the Advance Convoy 3 false starts and many days circular tour tossing the Bay of Biscay.

We have been kicking our heels in a beautiful village of St Remy du Plein – the scene of childhood days of Joan of Arc. Remy lies in the lovely hills and wooded country of the Somme area. The village only has one steep street of clean whitewashed houses.

"Stewy" Clemson, the battery cook has been lobbing stew and Army biscuits up at us for 3 weeks. They say "Stewy" Clemson cannot even boil water without him burning it.

We are getting used to the values of French Francs, Cents and Centimes. Most of my money has gone on "pain du buerre". The old baker has never sold so much before. He weighs the fresh hot bread, smears a coating of white butter on it and hands it over for your Franc 3:50.

The village has 4 cafés. Drinking wines from strange coloured bottles and lapping up Dubonnet, Cointreau and Citroen all night puts everybody in a singing mood. It's fortunate that Madame and others can't understand the bawdy Army choruses polluting the air. The air is thick with smoke for the French don't understand ventilation and these French cigarettes throw off as much smoke as a wet burning straw stack.

As Joe and myself left the café that final night, the cool night air slapped us and the floor seemed to come up and smack us in the face. I was drunk for the first time in my life but by hugging the house walls, first one side of the street then the other, we eventually reached our billet at the top end of the village. The wine together with the apples we had eaten from the nearby orchards gripped my stomach. Next morning, on firewood fatigues, I had to make many hasty excursions to drop my pants behind the nearest bush.

We are now ready to go to the front where we expect the Germans to start their scrap. Meanwhile, with so many "drunks" resulting from French wines, we are now only allowed to buy certain drinks. It is harvest time in this part of rural France, the roads between endless avenues of poplar trees, run for miles through orchard groves and fruit plantations. The ground crops are ready for picking too. However, we have been warned of eating any uncooked vegetables, for the French have the economical habit of fertilising their potatoes and cabbages with human manure.

The weather is now getting nippy night and morning and the sunny days are now intermingled with wet gusty days. Winter is on its way.

December 1939 : ORCHEES

For 5 months now we have been digging gun positions along the Belgium Frontier country. This is a miserable part of France. The land is flat and treeless. Most of the time heavy rain-soaked wind had been blowing across the open fields. Now that the snow has come, we have been rid of the misery of slushing about knee deep in the quagmire which represented our gun position. We have seen plenty of France, Rheims, Lille, Douai, as well as the endless villages in which we have been billeted. The Franco-German frontier has its Maginot Line but the Belgium Frontier was, at first, as unfortified as in 1914. Now the Infantry have dug out intricate trench systems, the French have constructed super tank traps and we have dug endless gun pits for the war which hasn't yet come.

We have been getting Anti-Invasion Manoeuvres manning the guns 3 days right off, firing blanks and getting soaked, mud-sodden and frozen. We have been learning Static-war conditions. The whole Division along the Frontier is doing the same. The DLI and Guards in front of us are doing their stuff too. The Paramount Newsreel man had his camera on "B" Troop a long time, getting his material to thrill the people at the cinemas back home on a make-believe war – until the real one turns up.

I hope it comes in warmer weather than this.

ORCHEES : On "Guards"

Shivering on guard once more. These gun guards come round every third night. 500 yards in front, hardly visible through the gloom, lies "A" Troop position, well sandbagged and camouflaged among a clump of trees. They had some excitement on their position last night, strange shadows among the guns, an unanswered challenge from the sentry and shots that sent two figures running across the fields.

Alongside runs the cobbled Frontier road, which runs straight on into Belgium. To my right is "B" Troop billet. It is a lonely bungalow and they should be quite comfortable compared to us. Our billet is a loft. The furniture in their bungalow is all under Police Impound, for Wiedeman - the French Bluebeard Murderer - committed his last 3 murders in the place before his arrest.

Our own gun position is on a farm, and the only person pottering about here most days and nights is the Polish refugee girl working here for her keep.

Behind is the railway line, and the dark silhouette of the cemetry and headstones denotes where the Third Troop position lies.

From the air, this position should be hidden by our camouflage, from the Nazi reconnaissance plane which flies over every morning. Our own aerial photos of the position show the gunpits only as 4 little blobs. But the print also shows a white circle round each blob and a white line threading it's way from each blob to the road. The white lines are the tracks (hardly visible on the ground) of our feet as we walk to and fro to the guns.

Those blobs, on the photo in the German Intelligence Room, will be plainly read as gunpits – given away by those white tell tale lines.

No slacking on Guard tonight. Geddes is Orderly Officer so the sentry had better patrol constantly through the 50 or 100 yards of inky blackness muffling the gun position, stumbling against barbed wire and falling down potholes of mud.

You see, knowing Geddes, he will make a half mile detour across black fields, sometime about midnight, and come onto the gun position from the blind side farthest from the sentry stand. Woe betide the sentry if Geddes can take away some small item from the guns without being seen or challenged. A sentry is responsible for all Government property on the beat, so the sentry had better keep moving if he values his skin - tonight at any rate.

Last night Richardson was Orderly Officer. He drove up from the main road with headlights full on. He turned out the Guard. He checked a man here, belt too loose; he checked a man there, respirator could be higher, he drubbed the men down for not being smart enough. Then off he went without noticing something more important than loose belts, low respirators or clicking heels. The Guard had turned out one man short! The missing man was warming his belly with coffee and rum in the farmhouse back parlour. Bullshit Baffled Brains.

Chapter Three

February to March 1940
LEAVE

Feb 22 : At 8 o'clock, 8 of us left RHQ. Not much room for 8 men and kit in 15cwt. Plenty of ice on the roads. Waited till midnight with about 2,000 others from units all over France. Much scrambling when the train eventually arrived (at the wrong platform). Rifles slung crosswise are most awkward things with which to get into a crowded compartment. Fully expected seeing somebody's eye dangling from the end of one, for everybody got jabbed in the face by somebody else's in the confusion of bagging sleeping space on the wooden seats. Too cold for sleep. Arrived Boulogne 5am. Catch boat 9am.

Feb 23 : Arrived Dover 10.20. Glad to leave stink of bilge and engine oil from the bowels of the ship. Weren't allowed up on deck (precautions against something). Glad to arrive Victoria. Fine seeing decent pavements again, (not cobbles) and decent buses, hearing London voices and handling familiar money. Surprised Mum and Dad when I burst indoors. Bathed and in civvies within half hour of arriving. Tom has bagged my shoes. Dad pleased with the bottles of French rum (Rhum) I brought home and Mum enjoyed her Sherry.

Feb 24 : Hard to leave the clean sheets this morning. Tom still in ARP. Mr Long is Warden now. Had a walk around the West End over my old Sunday nights' stroll.

Feb 25 : Paid call over the "Ocean". Saw Jacobs. Tom likes his new job at Mark Lane Branch. On evening took Lilly to The Palladium to see The Crazy Gang. Enjoyed "Mr Franklin D Roosevelt Jones". Had good laugh. Noticed West End has new black-out lighting – street lamps showing same amount of illumination as did the street lamps of 1750.

Feb 26 : Mum's birthday. Went to the Trocodero with Mum and Dad seeing "When the Rains Came". Later visited Mrs Kneen, 48 The Avenue, Cheam. Mrs Kneen pleased to see me. Winnie was away visiting her mother.

Feb 27 : Went to Aunt Lil's. Uncle Jack kept up a very enjoyable evening – "Coppernob" so-called because of her copper-coloured hair, is now engaged. Took Mum and Dad to Regal – saw Bing Crosby.

Feb 28 : On night visited Joe's Mother to pass her his message. Not a bad sister has Joe. Tom calls her "Kittenface".

Feb 29 : Dad, Lil and myself went to Eltham to see John and Marge. John working spare time with the Demolition Squad. Took "Kittenface" to the Majestic.

March 2 : Spent evening with Pheobe and George at their new house at Clapham. George now an ARP warden. Mum, Rose, Lil, Ted, and Tom came down later.

March 3 : We went down to Lou at Dulwich. Had tea – evening with cards.

March 4 : Caught 9 o'clock morning train from Victoria. Quickest 10 days I've known. Lilly, Mum and Tom (carrying my kit) came with me to the station. What a feeling this going back is. Platforms are crowded with returning British Expeditionary Forces (BEF) men with their relatives. Three trains are due to take us back to France but everybody is letting the first two trains go. All are waiting to catch the last. Feeling inwardly very miserable at going back again. The station loudspeakers at last succeed in hurrying the last goodbyes. General rush for the last train. Now realise I wasted my leave with too much travelling in all directions paying visits. I vow to make more of my next leave.

Chapter Four

April 1940
END OF LEAVE – NOW TO ARMENTIERS

We were billeted in Armentiers for 4 months. We arrived on the last day of December when frozen snow lay 5 inches deep on the ground. We left in April when bright spring sunshine was making the town a bright and cheerful place.

For on bright Sunday evenings, the young Madamoiselles, usually chaperoned by their Mothers, practiced the continental habit of promenading up and down the town high streets in their best clothes.

Armentiers was a typical French town with an impressive Town Hall, built similar to a Cathedral, standing in the centre of the Main Square. In front stood a fine bronze War Memorial to the French and Belgian civilians shot during the Great War (1914-18) by the Germans for aiding Allied Troops.

The main road Rue Nationale had 3 cinemas which showed American films for the British Troops billeted in the town.

The 92nd were billeted in "troops" all over the town. My

own billet was in an empty house in the Place Thiers. 4 men to each room and we felt quite at home, the best billets we have yet had in France. Most of us became keen customers to the neighbouring Patisserie, but it is hard to decide which was the main attraction, the luscious cream horns and puff pastries, or beautiful 17 year old Yvonne who sold them.

Sunday night was the night we "went to town" – the most popular place being the Café Univers. Many a pleasant Sunday evening Joe and myself drunk ourselves to that merry carefree state of intoxication, when nothing mattered and even BSM Ellis seemed, in our benevolent mood, as something human.

The Café Univers had a large hall-like interior with an accordion and string orchestra at one end. Along one side ran the long bar over which hundreds of Francs were spent every Sunday night in exchange for the deep red wines of Dubonnet, the Syrupy Citroen, the black "Tommy Stouts" and the light lagers and vin blancs. Hot meat rolls, eggs and chips were also sold to soak up the beer in the Tommies' bellies, for since the English troops had come to town, the Univers had had it's first drunken disorder. For a time the café had been out of bounds to British Troops ever since the HLI (Highland Light Infantry) had started a bottle fight with the 92nd.

The floor was usually crowded with small tables for 4 and family sixes. Every table had always its full complement, French Papa (if he was home from the Maginot), Madame and usually her fashionably dressed daughters. A charming daughter always meant free beer to the family from the Tommy, in order to get well in with the daughter, would also have to buy the rest of the family Cointreaus and

Dubonnets at Francs 2:50 a time. The French soldier is poorly paid and normally they would sit over a glass of wine all night. But with Tommy, trying to get beautiful Marianne, Papa and Mama can drink their free wine freely. Easy Come Easy Go. Their glasses are many times bottoms up. Vive l'Angleterre.

But when the café closes, Tommy must say goodnight to Marianne at once. Mama and Papa remember the British Troops in Armentiers in the last War, and so they see Marianne safely home. French girls are nothing like what we expected from this reputation.

Whilst we were in Armentiers we had our guns parked in a vast storage depot which served as an excellent Regimental Gunpark. Limber gunners and drivers worked all day on their maintenance whilst the remainder worked in working parties preparing more gun positions at Lincelles some 3 miles outside the town.

During these cold months, with the civilians on 3 meatless and coal less days a week, we often had them queuing for "buckshees" round our cookhouse.

I think this part of France has never recovered itself from the last war. Some of the houses still have shell holes in their walls, the roads are cobbled and paved with odd pavements. There is no sewerage and dogs are still used to pull light carts. We often saw French Army motor transport pass through - every other lorry being towed to save petrol. The Army still use horses – often blue uniformed cavalry come through. France is a poor country, the only thing rich in quality being their pastries and wines. I took plenty of wine home on my leave, but as regards French cigarettes, beer and their chocolate – the least said the better. And I have yet to see a French soldier clean shaven or march in step.

April 1940 : FRONTIER GUARDS

The Germans broadcast propaganda to one of the French regiments in the Maginot Line. It said "Whilst you are here in the front line - here with the danger of shot or shell, your gallant British allies are up in the North drinking and stealing your wives".

The French regiment replied "Who Cares? We come from the South".

But that propaganda made the British HQ act. They decided it would be better if we too did a spell in the Maginot. Accordingly, the HLI, DLI and Green Howards left Armentiers for the Maginot Line and the Artillery did their work of guarding frontier bridges. For 28 days the 92nd became Infantry. I enjoyed some of the work. Maybe only 3 men and 1 NCO would be stationed all alone for 3 days in some lonely Railway shed or on a Canal lock. Maybe 20 of us were in a Power Station. I used to prefer Power Station guards for it meant an opportunity of using their hot shower baths – quite a luxury to us. My worst Infantry Guard was during a blizzard (temp 28° below zero) on a bridge over a frozen canal. The canal ran through a village. The half of the village the far side of the bridge was in Belgium. At night, they had no blackout. Shop windows and lamps were burning brightly. They were neutral. Our side of the bridge was black. We were at War.

LINCELLES

At Lincelles, we are digging the best position we have yet done. We are in a farm. At the back of the farm are concrete pillboxes, relics of the German Hindenburg Line. Our guns will be concealed along the front of the farm. As we work here all day, we each give 5 Francs to the farmer's wife and she cooks us a midday meal of lentil soup, garlic, fried eggs and chips, red wine and bread and butter.

Our first gun pit is cut out in a straw shed. My gun will be concealed inside a dummy haystack which we are constructing. The front of the stack will roll aside when we fire. The third gun peeps out of a sty, the fourth looks like a shrub. All four guns are perfectly camouflaged. No-one would dream this was a gun position.

Captain Aris flies over the position in an RAF Lysander to see how effective our work is. In a field in front of the guns, hardly noticeable on the ground but distinctly visible from the air, is a large figure 5 (our regimental serial number) traced out on the ground in white ash. That white ash 5 has betrayed us. It has shown the German reconnaissance plane - which comes over every morning - that behind that "5" concealed in the farm sheds is a 4 gun troop position belonging to the 92nd Field Regiment. It is my first experience of 5th column work. We rather suspect the farmer.

May 1940 : BEAUVAIS

With the closing days of April, the 5th Division left the Armentiers area, the flat country of Northern France, to do 10 days intensive Divisional Training in the hills and wooded country of the Outer Somme Valley.

The Division has been waiting for 7 months on the frontier waiting for the war to come to us. Hitler had made a few alarming troop concentrations on the Lowlands borders but apart from cancelling BEF leave, it didn't fetch the fireworks any nearer.

And so now the 5th are to do a little heavy training, leave the gentleman's war in France and seek the war in the frozen woods and lakes of Norway. There, a BEF up to its knees in snow, is trying to make a show against the German troops. The Nazis, dropped from the skies by parachute, are able to strike lightning attacks, over the snow on skies and snowshoes. Meanwhile, the BEF (made up from new militiamen) is bogged well and truly, and the latest reinforcements have arrived in time to start destroying our equipment in the docks and to drive the AA guns and vehicles over the fiords into the torrents below. The evacuation from Norway has almost started.

By the time we finish our 10 day training and get to the port of Le Havre for embarkation, the Norway Campaign is finished.

Left in Beauvais on hearing this news, I hope we will spend some time in this pleasant part of France. I do a little sight seeing in Beauvais. The town itself reminds me of the Californian towns that one sees on the movies.

The roads are wide and good. The pavements are also wide and very clean. Down each pavement alongside the road, on a 6ft wide grass verge, runs an avenue of tall Yew trees, shading the roads. The houses on either side stand in their own gardens. Front gardens I have rarely seen in France.

I visited the Cathedral, inside is a marvellous model, 10ft square standing under glass. It was built 800 years ago and consists of a multi-information model. A bronze clock forms the front of the model. It is wound up only once every hundred years. It tells, not only the time, but also the day month and year. At the back is a working model of the paths of the stars and moon. From this year you can tell the position of the constellations and the date of the next full moon. Other parts of the piece show you if the sea is smooth or rough, what weather you are having or what you will have.

Outside the town is the hill into which Britain's ill-fated R101 buried itself in flames taking with it many lives (including some of the air staff).

Coming back to where our guns are lining the road, I find the rest of the gunners talking excitedly in little groups. "Germany has invaded Belgium and Holland". Those Jerry planes we heard last night had bombed Nantes.

Chapter Five

27 May 1940
ASPELAERE (10 Miles outside Brussels)

We are dug in as first line defence on Brussels. Each gun muzzle peeps through the hedge of the back garden.

We worked late last night, digging well, down 2 feet and across 15 feet in diameter, and sandbagging 3 feet high as splinter proof protection. A deeper trench serves as an ammo trench. 150 rounds of 25 pounder HE is no healthy thing to have around in the gunpit. Over all is the camouflage netting which caused us so much swearing as we put it up in the dark.

And now the gun is manned on it's platform in the pit, muzzle peeping through the hedge, is ready for the first fire order.

Yesterday for 9 hours, we were part of the mechanised BEF column which was trying hard to get as far into Belgium as was possible against the oncoming flood of wretched Belgium refugees. The fast moving German advance motor cycle units, travelling at 45mph, had been arriving in the Belgian villages hours ahead of the German army. The villagers immediately had thought the Army had arrived and fled with as much of their homes as could be piled onto a barrow. Refugees are Hitler's ally. He throngs as many thousands as possible onto the roads and drives them against the BEF columns of guns, tanks, tractors and transport.

The procession of prams, overloaded carts, barrows, men, women and howling children was at least 12 miles long up to the time we reached our sector. As we passed through the bombed town of Tournai, I saw my first crashed German plane piled nose down on the pavement. Progress of the BEF column was very slow for very often the crazily loaded prams or carts would overturn and the excitable peasants and crowding sympathisers would cause so great a block that for nearly an hour the BEF column would be held at a standstill.

At one long halt, I practiced my schoolboy French on a Belgian with a bandaged arm, standing beside his farm cart which leaned crazily on its broken wheel.

In French and English he told me his tale...."The roads were choked with the civilians fleeing from the oncoming Germans. Over the packed roads came a low flying aeroplane flying English markings. The peasants stopped and waved, cheered 'Vive L'Allies' and then before they realised it, the plane had started spraying machine gun bullets into them. The old man had lost his daughter in that butchery and got a bullet lodged in his arm. His wife is lost in the crowd, and now his cart has broken down".

The order came "Get mounted". I had to run for my tractor. No wonder the poor wretches scramble for the ditches every time they hear planes. They cannot trust rules in this warfare. Even uniforms of one side are being worn by the other.

Hitler, rightly or wrongly, believes in TOTAL war.

THE FIRST POSITION

About 4 o'clock yesterday, the convoy started thinning out as different regiments took up their respective battle positions. We had reached our zone and had hurried a hot meal of stew and pepper. It tasted like a meal of pepper with stew added.

Even now, a constant drumming and crashing of ack ack, bombs and shells told us that the front line troops were already being engaged. Nazi bombers had already started spraying the aerodrome alongside us, with very marked attention. Screaming dive bombers sent us scrambling into the thickets, on and off for the last few hours of daylight. As night fell, we took over our troop position and dug in. We were to be second line defence on Brussels.

I clicked for gunguard that night. All night long, the horizon in front was vivid with flashes and the crashing of shells. The thunderings and flashes seemed to be jumping throughout the night, ever nearer and closer. Soon the chatter of small arms fire could be heard too, crackling among the din.

Low rumbling on the road alongside us some 100 yards away, transport was on the move. I felt relived too, to think that fresh troops were going up. Maybe then, that front line would not bear down on us so quickly.

What a surprise when someone, coming onto the gun position brought the news that the medium batteries, who had been firing in front of us, were pulling out. And that rumbling we could hear was the infantry bren gun carriers of the Guards and Green Howards fetching men from the line – an organised withdrawal.

By breakfast time we were first line artillery waiting for the first target.

It comes. German infantry trying to build pontoons across the River Dendre. I was doing N° 2, slamming the breech, setting the range, N° 3's ready – FIRE – the gunpiece leaped back with an earsplitting crack, and the breech was open again, throwing out the red hot cartridge case and ready for the next. We laughed to cover our excitement. We were actually in action.

But so far we only had the muck going one direction. Not for long though. Within 20 minutes of first firing, 3 Messerschmidts zoomed from the sky, shot down a Lysander circling above us (the last RAF plane I would see for a month), and then crisscrossed our position splattering the guns with bullets.

This was our baptism of fire, and the Law of Self Preservation proved stronger than a series of Fire Orders. We made very un-soldierly-like scrambles for our slit trenches. Sgt Tinker in the next troop position was more of a soldier. He kept at his position at his guntrail. Sgt Tinker thus became our first fatal casualty. Lt Middleton and RSM Ellis slanged us right and left for leaving the guns and we hurriedly recovered ourselves to take post again.

The whole day and night we sent hundreds of shells over onto infantry, transport and bridges. The din during the day was terrific. The screaming of dive bombers, the thud of bombs, the woof of howitzers, the crack of 25 pounders and the door slamming of heavy 3.7 ack ack all in one concert of noise. The dive bombers fortunately for us were paying their attention to the ack ack batteries. By dusk, the ack ack had all withdrawn and the absence of their comforting barrage brought home the realisation that our only defence from the air now was the bren guns on our flank.

Whom. Whom. Whom. Whom. Four white puffs of smoke appeared in line among the trees in front of us some 100 yards away. I never knew we had any guns positions in front of us, firing. Whoom. There they fire again. At the second whoom, a tree rose in the billow of smoke and crashed sideways. Hell ! That must be German artillery searching for us. They have soon suspected our whereabouts.

The night became vivid as we fired 300 rounds a gun onto German troops pouring over the canal. The guards were falling back leaving only their covering platoons. By breakfast, we too pulled out, troop at a time, just as the shells are beginning to pound our position. We were glad to leave them. The front was strategically withdrawing.

SOUTH OF BEAURAINS

The Troop is having a fine rest here, whilst waiting for all the regiment to find itself again. Billeted here in this deserted village, we are living on the fat of the land, and already 30 chickens have gone in the stew pot in 3 days for the Troop of 60 men. The cows are lowing miserably – they have had nobody to milk them for 3 days or more. Starving dogs, released now from their chains for the first time since their puppy hood, are the only living things in the streets. The houses have long since been looted by the troops. I always have a pang of conscience, whenever I enter a house, and have seen the plates on the table from the last hurried meal before they fled, the photos on the wall of wedding groups, portraits and family groups.

I never take anything, unless perhaps soap or necessities.

Before our flight home, we had been firmly dug in on Vimy Ridge. The towers of the white Canadian War Memorial, standing among the war cemeteries of the thousands of Canadian Fallen of 25 years ago, were now serving as excellent G.A.Ps for our guns. Below us in Vimy en Vele, where we had been bombed on the road as we were coming into position, was the same familiar creeping columns of wretched refugees, swollen now by thousands from Northern France.

French front line troops were straggling back with pessimistic expressions. French Tanks were coming back too. One stopped with engine trouble. Without stopping to attempt it's repair, the crew destroyed it, burning it with it's own petrol.

From dawn to dusk, formations of German bombers and fighters, 200 and 250 strong were systematically destroying allied points of resistance, French towns, anybody or troops worthy of attention. What the German tank could not pass, the dive bombers were destroying for it. I have heard they are in radio communication with one another.

We were told we were moving forward to Arras. The D.L.I and Manchester machine gunners had cleared the town of Germans and we were going to help in mopping up operations. But as we came nearer to Arras, we found French and British machine gunners, mounted on sidecars, lining the roads for a mile outside the town.

Arras was being systematically destroyed by incendiary and H.E. Hardly bothering with the mile and a half column of our guns, and tractors, along the road, Nazi dive bombers were circling over the town, and then pulling off to fall, one after another, in a vertical drive and release their load on the houses below. We watched the houses going up in clouds of black dust and smoke and then begin to blaze up as the incendiaries got to work.

Then as we moved up nearer to take up positions, the cross roads became a target for Nazi field artillery. At regular minute intervals, salvoes crashed onto the stretch of crossing, but by each vehicle accelerating over the unhealthy stretch between the regular shell bursts, we safely reached our dispersing area. Each troop made off for it's position.

As the night wore on, the black pall above Arras turned a fiery red, until the whole town seemed an inferno. The many haystacks around us too were burning, white hot beacons fired by Nazi incendiary bullets during the day, presumably to serve as guiding beacons to their troops at night.

We had heard from the infantry that the Germans had already thrust a mechanised column down to Boulogne. We felt very insecure as night went on for the Nazis white success rockets were shooting up in the sky, seemingly all round us. It was satisfying when we fired on one target to see a white glow billow up, followed by an explosion. And as we pounded the target, so the glow leaped higher and turned crimson. It was satisfying to know we were doing something.

"Tank Alert !" We hurriedly loaded A.P ammo and waited.

Presently, a tank came charging the position – firing white tracer shells. We held heavy fire although small arms opened up. Fortunately for tank and us, it proved to be a French tank mistaking us for Nazis. Mistakes were easy in this war of movement with a front everywhere and anywhere. We got the order to withdraw, every troop independently! Those white rockets had long told us we were encircled. Now we had to get out as best we could. We formed along the road and moved back the way we came. As we passed trough the town of Lens, the city was glowing with burning factories.

Dead civilians and horses with shrapnel tears in their bellies were littering the roads. It seems a dead city. A shout, and we were stopping to pick up just 3 from a British tank crew. They were the only survivors of their tank squadron, and as we clattered along, they told us boiling stories of the German method of war, of tanks against civilians. We were not hard to convince. We had already seen at the corner of the street the bodies of a family machine gunned against a wall as they stood, held immobile before a diving plane.

"The Germans", our passengers told us, "were in the town". As we came to the outskirts where the road ran into the open fields again, we got a nasty setback. Across the roads were barricades of overturned farm carts erected by the fleeing farmers as stumbling blocks to the Nazis. We hurriedly cleared away the first but when, a few hundred yards later, we encountered a second, we were more than annoyed. Lt Middleton decided to waste no further time.

Leading the column of guns, we drove off the road and over the fields, rough riding over ground which we would have avoided normally. The fact that the fields of Northern

France have no hedges saved us. We drove some 50 miles to a reorganising point. I now realise how flat France has always been the cockpit of all the battles of Europe. No country is better suited for moving large bodies of men over large areas. If hedges had lined the fields, that night might well have seen us overtaken as we cleared the barricades.

These 3 days that we waited until the regiment came together again have been a godsend. We have had much needed baths, and have had some excellent food.

By the time Lt Middleton comes back to us with news of the whereabouts of the rest of the regiment, the village has become swept into the war area.

As we pull out to join the main body, shells have already started falling along the road. The war soon catches up with you in this style of war. Blitz Krieg lives up to it's name.

AT DICKEBUSCH (Near Ypres)

In actual fact, I had been sleeping fully 3 hours. But when Sgt Drake gave me a shrug, it had only seemed like ¼ of an hour.

I got myself slowly out of the clean sheets of the most comfortable bed in the world. Huge clods of mud still stuck to the sheets as I withdrew my muddy booted feet from last night's virgin whiteness. What did it matter if I had slept in the bed fully clothed. I hadn't had my boots off for any length of time for 3 weeks and in any case, the house, bed and everything, would in all probability be destroyed or fall in German hands very shortly.

In the back garden stood our 25 pounder, in it's nearly

completed gun pit. Filling sandbags all night hadn't improved my miserable outlook on life.

For 3 weeks we have been fighting from Brussels, to Beauvais, and once back more into Belgium where we now hoped to make a stand at Ypres.

This war moves too quickly. By day, we fire and are fired on, are kept busy unloading ammo and forever wondering when those eternal planes up there, overhead, are going to blast us to 'kingdom come'. Nightfall brings respite from bombers but not for us. For at night, under cover of darkness, we will move to our next position. The line is always withdrawing to prevent being outflanked. The tractors, as silently as their engines will allow them, will come up to us from the Wagon Lines, we will limber up, hook in and climb sleepily into the tractor.

For the short time it takes us to reach our new position, I will sleep soundly. But all too soon, we will be tumbling out again. Same old routine. Unhook! The tractors will vanish in the night bound for near Wagon Lines and sleep. For us ? Selecting the gun position. Cutting down that hedge or tree in the way of our 'field of fire'. Digging the pit, sandbagging the walls, hauling in the gun onto it's platform and then erecting the net. What the net does not camouflage, sprigs and bushes (uprooted and transplanted) will. Finally the slit trench. By this time, dawn would be creeping up and, tired or not, you would dig well, for day brings dive bombers. And how welcome is the slit trench then. Day brings fresh targets, shelling, bombs and nightfall will complete the cycle of events.

I tumbled out of the bed past that wretched dog, and down to the gun at the bottom of the garden. That chained dog was savage. It must be nearly starved for the villagers fled days ago. If I realised it, it would be dangerous for it couldn't find food. And yet I don't want to put a rifle bullet in it's head. A rifle bullet makes a mess and I know how a dog's brains can splash.

Rations aren't up yet – the third day too. Tennyson has killed a sheep for the Troops' breakfast. Bob Martin and myself wander off to milk a cow. We wander further and further afield – nearly to the next village. People here have started drifting back to the homes they so recently left. A white flag flutters from the church steeple. Sheets and tablecloths are coming out on broom handles from top floor windows.

"What's this", we ask a tired infantryman "Washing day ?". "Washing day be blowed! Belgium has surrendered !".

Chapter Six

OUTSIDE ADINKERKE
EN ROUTE FOR DUNKIRK

We had been told we were fighting a withdrawal to Dunkirk. People at home were praying for us – a National Day of Prayer for the BEF. The RAF were still conspicuous by it's absence and the Nazi pilots had recently dropped a lighter load than bombs on the troops. These loads of propaganda leaflets showed the map of Holland, Belgium and North France with practically the whole of the land area criss crossed with Swastikas. I say practically, for in that Swastika forest was a small area marked BEF surrounding a small Dunkirk.

Overleaf they appealed to us "Come Tommies. You have played the match and lost. You are surrounded. Lay down your Arms. We take prisoners. Come and see for yourselves what decent chaps we are!". Not a very cheerful prospect for us.

We had our guns loopholing the farmyard walls. The chicken house immediately alongside was serving admirably as a storehouse for our 300 rounds of ammo.

On the road alongside, next to the canal, detachments of infantry machine gunners were already dug in. Their guns were noisily contributing to the chattering of small arms fire already sounding from the wood thickets half a mile in front of us. As we fired into the village where enemy troops were concentrating, I threw two of the ejected cartridge cases aside for packing in my valise. If ever I get away from this safely, I thought, these brass cases will polish up well and will make fine souvenirs as they stand each end in the fire hearth.

Bits of the church steeple jumped away in dusty clouds of smoke in answer to our gun fire. In the belfry of that church was a German OP officer spotting for his troops.

Did he really see the muzzles of our guns, barely peeping through the wall, or was he attracted by our thoughtless signallers who were foolishly trying to ride those cavalry horses abandoned by the surrendering Belgians. Pew – whoof ! A salvo landed in front of us. Minus. Pew – whoof. A salvo in rear of us. Plus. We were in a bracket crack !! No preliminary whistle of the shells that time. The nearer you are to landing shells, the shorter the warning whine. We were clearly on the receiving end this time. Fred Portwaine's quad leapt sideways and burst into flames.

Left 10 inches. George Baldwin traversed the gun and fired. There came a flash, a crack and something kicked my elbow. The hen house alongside was beginning to blaze – and 300 rounds of ammo stored there!

We immediately started pulling out the trays of ammo but when I went to reach out, my left arm would not respond. Looking at my hand I saw a trickling stream of blood running from my sleeve. Hell ! I've kidded myself all along I would come through without a scratch, and this from our own shell too. But as I removed my overcoat, a wicked gash across the back of it showed I had missed more than I had collected.

Walking back along the road to the Aid Post in the farmhouse, I heard a voice alongside shout "Down!" Obediently I ducked and was almost pushed over by a blast of hot air. Four express trains were tearing through the air above my head. I had forgotten B Troop's gun position was dug in just off the road here. They were dug down, their muzzles just above ground level. And already they were firing their second salvo. Somebody was getting it hot.

The farmhouse served as a Command Post as well as the Aid Post. After my elbow was dressed, Major Cragg-Hamilton gave me a drop of brandy and asked me if I cared to make my way to the CCS. "No thank you Sir, I'd rather keep with the unit". What a wise choice I made, for Sgt Maylin, also wounded - to keep with the unit, had to go to the CCS. And when the CCS had fallen into the German's hands, Sgt Maylin became a Prisoner of War.

As I left the building to return, L/Bdr Bull – Cragg-Hamilton's batman, was packing essential kit on their last dash for Dunkirk – and England. But nobody in the Command Post saw England. So soon after I left it, the farmhouse was but a heap of rubble, dust and stinking cordite fumes.

They say Major Cragg-Hamilton died a hero. With one leg severed, he shouted encouragement to the gunners until the next shells finished their work.

'A' Troop lost all it's guns in the next quarter of an hour and a number of signallers too, who were foolishly sent to do what the gunners had decided could not be done. And that was to pull a gun from it's pit which was being demolished by shellfire.

With signallers lines to our troop position shattered, we waited in vain for our next orders. At last a withdrawal order came by runner. Our infantry were already trickling back as we moved out and the German gunners obligingly switched onto the road as we got onto it. One tractor was all they bagged along the road.

With 8 guns left in 24, the regiment was taking up a regimental gun position just outside Dunkirk. They were to be honoured as the last Artillery to come away from Dunkirk. With only 8 guns, all surplus men were set to destroying equipment, truck and wireless sets before being sent on to the beaches.

I went to the CCS in the town. For the past ten miles, I had seen the biggest wilful destruction ever witnessed. The road had a canal alongside it's length. Into this were pushed thousands of tanks, trucks, heavy lorries, motor cycles and stores. Along the road flocked infantrymen with only their riffles and ammo, artillerymen, their guns either destroyed by the Germans or themselves, French troops, stragglers and deserters. All were flocking to the port which might mean Salvation.

Over that port, hung a black pall of smoke. Every building burned and contributed it's column of smoke to that blanket overhanging the city. Overhead droned huge formations of bombers. They hardly bothered about the columns of human ants below. They, high in the heavens, like the procession far below, were all bound for one place – Dunkirk. Once over the town they poured their loads into the burning city, onto crumbling buildings and the armies threading it's streets.

The lighter planes would be strafing the beaches. Once, during these last few miles, I had seen an anti-tank battery going up to the front. I felt something inside me go out to them – they alone going up to meet an enemy when it seemed the rest of the whole Army was flocking against them – away from the enemy. But of course, they with the other infantry units who would be holding the line, would only be doing what everyone else had done in turn. Someone must hold the line long enough for the others to withdraw. The 92nd were preparing to hold the last and smallest circle formed round Dunkirk.

I was watching the RAF in action for the first time. A squadron was engaging the bombers over the town. I saw one plane peel off, and fall slowly, spiralling like a falling leaf. It left a trail of black smoke in the sky. How we cheered. Was it theirs or ours? We hardly knew. But it was such a tonic to see those bombers at last, getting engaged after a whole month's monopoly of the sky that it hardly mattered whose plane it was falling.

Chapter Seven

1 June 1940
DUNKIRK

As darkness fell, the black canopy over the town gradually turned fiery red. In the reflected red glow, I found the CCS in a mansion standing in it's own grounds it's windows shuttered and doors curtained off.

That night in a CCS will remain an indelible memory.

In the hall, they take my name, number and unit. An orderly takes me to a back room. "Some more chaps from your unit in here" he says.

There is Dvr Thrift. He got his in both legs when a shell burst in front of his truck. There is Sig Gidden and a couple more. I forget their names. The others about the room are in sad states.

I feel ashamed to be in here with only an arm wound. The orderlies work quickly and silently. With the next tide in the morning they hope to get away. A chap on a stretcher moans for morphine. An orderly pricks his arm with an empty needle. Satisfied the patient quietens. It's useless asking for water. The town had it's water mains bombed days ago.

In dim light of candles they move among the wounded, dressing new wounds but leaving those with field dressings. Now that nightfall has chased the bombers from the sky, shells are carrying on the work. Most of them are whining right over us, bound for the docks and waterfront. But a number crash without warning in the gardens outside. A cry of a badly wounded man fearing further wounds is not easily forgotten.

With the dawn came ambulances to take us to the docks. With the first of daylight came the bombers again. And with the coming of light, the fiery red smoke pall over the town assumes once more blackness. The ugly red will not return again till nightfall. By then I hope to be away.

The ambulances did not get far. Rubble and debris across the street prevented it. We piled out and helped the less fortunate who couldn't walk. I had my right arm round the waist of a RAOC Sergeant who only had boots and trousers on. His many bandages about his body still dripped blood.

As we passed a mobile Bofors AA it started its rhythmic coughing as it pumped its clip of shells into the low blanket of smoke over the town. And out of the smoke pall, dived a plane spraying the streets with bullets.

A MP advised us to make for the Mole. "You won't stand a chance on the beaches" he said, "They've been shelling and bombing them for a week. There's thousands been waiting on them for days".

I don't know how we came to the Mole for nobody could even direct us to the waterfront. The Mole too was under shellfire. A hole almost divided the concrete jetty in two.

Greatcoats covered the faces of those who had managed to get this far, but not far enough.

A long queue of French and British extended the whole length of the Mole – as orderly as a theatre queue.

On the beach, crocodiles of men wound in and around itself like coiled snakes, the heads of which finished up out in the sea. There, small boats were unceremoniously loading them in – almost to the danger of capsizing.

Destroyers were against the Mole side. After 3 hours in the queue, I tumbled onto the deck of H34. The decks were crowded with troops. In the bay, the mast of a sunken destroyer stuck up out of the water. "How many went down with her" I wondered. But I have always had great confidence in the Navy and now I was aboard a naval vessel, I could sit down and drink that hot tea a Tar was passing round among us.

We pulled away to sea, away from the hellish din of bombs, bullets and shells, to which I had grown so accustomed to these past few weeks. As I watched burning Dunkirk on the horizon 5 miles away, I had my musings rudely shattered by the ships noisy 2lb pom-poms. Our companion destroyer also gave all it could to the noisy concert. A Nazi plane, which had ventured far out to sea for a last desperate attempt at machine gunning crowded decks hit the water with a splash. We never tarried to pick up survivors.

Chapter Eight
WALES, ENGLAND, SCOTLAND

June 1940
PORTHCAWL

867098 Gnr W Holt
c/o The Royal Welsh Fusiliers
The Miner's Rest Home
Porthcawl
Glamorganshire

23 June 1940

Dear Mum, Dad and all,

A hurried note for I will now shortly be rejoining the regiment at Knutsford, so don't answer this until you get my new address. Maybe then, I will get this much talked of King's Privilege 48 hours leave.

I'll be sorry to leave this place, - it's been good as a seaside holiday for me these past 3 weeks. The cinemas here are free to uniformed men and naturally I have taken full advantage of the privilege.

The Welsh people, here, have been very good to us since we arrived. You could not go for a walk along the promenade without a car pulling in to offer you a lift. I had my Sunday dinner out with some people who I got friendly with – it was great getting out and eating some roast lamb and green peas. I was glad the time we spent eating, did not allow much time for talking for I find it hard understanding their quick sing song dialect.

I am glad Len has been to see you. He has soon got his 48 hours King's Privilege leave, but of course, I won't get mine until I get back to my unit.

All well at present etc. etc. Will.

June 1940 : KNUTSFORD (NEAR MANCHESTER)

26 June : Left Tattham Park Estate (where the Division is under canvas) for Knutsford Station. Arrived just in time to be too late. Train was just gathering speed. 5 hours for next train. Did not want to waste the first 5 hours of my leave sitting on the platform bench watching the line of milk churns on the opposite platform. Decided to thumb a lorry to London. After 3 hours travelling between lorries and cars, found myself in Birmingham. Decided to use my rail ticket I had got from Knutsford to continue train journey from Birmingham. Little trouble with collector. Firstly my ticket says Knutsford, not Birmingham. Secondly this was LMS and my ticket was LNER. He let me through but wouldn't promise how I would fare at the other end. Rail journey in good time – 1 hour. Joined throng of passengers passing through gates, thrust my ticket in collector's hand which wasn't noticed in crowd. Arrived home. Mr Long opened door and very pleased to see me. Mum had just received letter from the War Office "regretting that Gnr Holt was wounded and his present whereabouts unknown". Good job I had written home first opportunity when I reached England!

27 – 28 June : Very enjoyable leave – made most of home comforts. My wardrobe of civvies is dwindling whilst I am in the Army. Tom has grown now and believes in saving my suits and mac from moths by wearing them. Dad has taken to wearing my collars and has made the startling discovery that my neck ties fit him as well as they do me.

29 June : Had Rose and Ted to dinner. Mum, Rose and Ted, Lil and Tom, the whole crowd came to see me off. Midnight train Kings X. Batch of our lads on the platform going back so I will have plenty of company. Very surprised to see McQuade. He is rejoining regiment. The last time we saw him was in Belgium when he went missing. Thought he was dead but he has been attaching himself to an Ack Ack mob. Some of the lads joking about him coming back from the dead, are punching him (not too gently) to see if he is a ghost.

As the time comes for boarding the train, I wish all goodbye and promise them I might shortly get the 7 days leave due to me.

7 July : FINTRAY, ABERDEENSHIRE
Have yet to see where the bonnie in "bonnie Scotland" fits in. Midsummer yet the sky is forever low and grey with a cold wind blowing. The one shop in Fintray village serves as Post Office and General Stores. Had a walk for 10 miles to nearest town (Dyce) to see what it is like. Arrived, stayed long enough to have a café tea, and walked back again, only seeing 2 persons on the way back.

Spent Saturday in Aberdeen – The Granite City. Fine

buildings and cinemas. Not quite the city I imagine it is in peacetime. The Aberdonians are hard to sort from the English troops and sailors thronging the streets. I always imagined Aberdeen as a city of kilts. A kilt seems so rare that even a Scotsman would turn to look at one being worn.

14 July : ALMONDBANK, NEAR PERTH

The regiment is being split up! A draught (including myself) will be joining a Scottish Yeomanry regiment which has just been converted from horse cavalry into artillery. Just as most units from the South of England are sprinkled around Scotland, so are many Scottish units down in the south. By joining this Yeomanry unit, I may stand a good chance of being stationed near home.

Almondbank is one of the prettiest places I've seen in Scotland. This place is much better than the bleak moors of peat and heather which I've only seen upto now. For the first time in my experience, I find the actual scenery up to the same standard as its own picture post card views in the post card racks of the village newsagents.

This little village has opened up a canteen for our benefit, in the Presbyterian church parlour. This is a very welcome and popular way of spending an evening hour after which most chaps dwindle off to win the hearts of the few village maidens. Ginger Whellams is making many rapid conquests, mostly on account of his recently won military medal ribbon on his chest. I would like to hear the yarns he spins around it.

The Laird of the Estate on which we have our camp pitched, has allowed us to fish in his lake. The lake has obviously been undisturbed for years for no sooner are lines cast than the catch is being hauled in. In no time, snapping pike are littering the bank. Their vicious teeth don't invite too much handling. Even when after a time, one seemed dead, it suddenly snapped at the hand about to pick it up. But boiled fish makes a welcome addition to the Army menu.

23 July 1940 : We have left the 92nd, the regiment I've been in since before I was 18, and have arrived at the county town of Lanark (30 miles from Glasgow). A reception committee of officers and sergeant majors, still wearing Cavalry Sam Brownes and jingling spurs, is awaiting our arrival on the platform. I fancy we cannot take a very favourable impression in our scruffy battledresses. The one I am wearing has already been condemned on parade as WS twice. I don't think I'll have long to wait for the hat trick to turn up.

August 1940 : A day in the Yeomanry (155)

5am — Reveille. Pitch dark. Trumpeter McCleary sits up in bed, reaches for his cavalry trumpet, puts it to his lips and blows a rousing Cavalry Reveille. I wake up.

5.5am — Brewer, from the lower half of the bunk, gives me a shrug. I wake up.

5.10am — Bdr Robson comes round to each bed in turn shouting "Show a leg". I wake up and oblige.

5.15am — Procession of bombardiers, orderly sergeant and sergeant majors, each in turn, come round banging their sticks. I am forced to wake up.

6am Shivering on the field doing 1 hour's gun drill with troop of guns (2 18 pounders different makes, 1 4.5 Howitzer and a French 75).

7am Breakfast – Scotch porridge with salt instead of sugar, causing international arguments over table. Tea, bread and kippers. 6 kippers per table but enough skins and fishbones left at end of meal to make a further 6 kippers per table.

8-12.30 Parade hours, lectures, gun drill and instruction. Feeling bored.

1pm Tea time. Tea, bread, tomatoes, cheese, jam.

2pm Further 1 hours instruction on things which are useful, might come in useful and useless, Feeling tired.

3pm Bed time. Everyone beds down, and sleeps.

6.30pm Dinner time, roast, potatoes, cremola and prunes.

10.30pm Lights out.

The nights in the Yeomanry (155 Field)

Monday night
A nights sleep in the billet.

Tuesday night
All nights circular route march to Carluke and bivowac out. Night under the stars.

Wednesday night

Parachute Picket. Stand To 10-11 night and 4-5 morning. 5 hours sleep in blanket on floor of the ex-stables, now serving as Ammo Store.

Thursday night

Thursday is Rest day. Most Scotsmen away to their local homes. Clear night in billet.

Friday night

Road block duty or Guard.

Saturday night

Clear night in billet.

Sunday night

Night spent in digging practice gun pits in dark.

General Purpose of night training is to accustom men to the night work of Active Service Conditions.

General Inference that my bed in the billet is only something to have made up neatly for billet inspections.

General Conclusion I dropped a goolie when I came to the unit expecting to better myself. The unit is recruited from the local district, is stationed here and looks like keeping here. Some men have sleeping out passes for their own homes. Bdr Bowman the Battery Office Clerk goes home 5 o'clock every night and comes to work again 9 o'clock next morning – practically a civvy job for some of them in the unit. And I am farther from home now (in miles) than I was when abroad.

At Beattock, where we were doing a fortnight's firing camp, I receive a disturbing letter from home. The air raids have started on London; Mr and Mrs Long are among the 24 people killed in the surface shelter at Ewer Street, hit by an aerial torpedo. Thank God Mum had never taken my advice to use that shelter. Our house has been badly shaken about too and is unsafe. The family after spending a day or two living in Grays' Street School now have a new place in Southwark Street.

The camp (the first since the regiment became Artillery) is a success. Plenty of manhandling guns through the gateways in the walled dykes dividing the moors into fields, and digging out trucks, sunk to their axles in the peat bogs. Shooting is good but fails to disturb the shaggy haired highland cattle which stand around in silent groups watching us like as if they leave better things than us behind the dykes.

30 September 1940 : Leave

My leave at last, overdue since June. Catch 10 o'clock train at Lanark arriving London 11 at night – 13 hours. As we drew near London, the train slows down to snail's pace in complete darkness. We can already see the areas of searchlight beams over London. The train moves so slowly and quietly that we can hear the drone of bombers. Flashes and explosions along the line – hope it was ack-ack. As train nears station and creeps along the last lap to Kings Cross, our faces at the window are scorched by 5 blazing coaches bombed on the siding alongside. London seems to be having another night of it.

Am seeing wartime London for the first time. Making my way down to the tube, have to pick my way gingerly over the women and kiddies trying to sleep in cramped sitting positions on the staircases. The platform is worse – whole families are bedded down on the floor. Cannot get beyond

Moorgate because the tube is closed under the river. Have a midnight walk through the deserted City area. As I cross Southwark Bridge, I see that the raid appears to be over our side of the river. I call in at Southwark Street shelter to find somebody, as I have not yet seen our new home. Cannot find any of the family among the sleeping bundles along the benches.

Am just leaving with the Shelter Marshall who has been helping me find any of the family when Lily, waking up, recognises my voice and calls me.

As soon as Lily starts crying, I know something has happened. Mum has now awakened. She asks me if I have received the Telegram she sent off to me. Of course not – I have come home on leave. I ask "Who is it"? but now before Mum tells me. Who else could it be? Tom ! my young brother.

1 October : I hear today how the warden's post was brought down in the bombing just as the 3am relief was taking over, thus burying 10 men where, 5 mins earlier, were only 5. Of the 10 men in the cellar, one was blown clear. The Rescue Squad was hampered as they couldn't use night flares. Young Tom's body was the last to be recovered some 24 hours later. Mrs Cheeseman's husband and son were both in the Post – this makes her 7th bereavement this war.

Went with Rose to see Tom at the Casualty Station.

6 October : The air raid sirens threatened to disturb the Memorial Service in Southwark Cathedral. The coffins are draped with Union Jacks and the AFS are acting as Pall Bearers. With this final loss, the whole of Southwark's original ARP squads are now gone. The civilians are suffering more this war than the Army.

7 October : In the train back to Scotland, returning from a memorable leave, I have with me Tom's last letter he wrote to me. He had never lived to post it.

It runs :

"Sept 27th 1940

Dear Will,
I have taken a night off tonight and am writing this letter in Southwark Street Shelter. Mum does not like the brick shelters which have been built for the buildings. But each night there are more people in the shelter and if it became too full, and I took a night off, I would go into the brick shelter as I rather prefer these to the shelters with big buildings above them. Phew !

When I go to the Post, I have a sleep but not a very good one as it is rather cold and an old door is not an ideal place for sleeping.

At work, Ropemaker Street has not been open this last week and HO are being paid at the rate of 2/- a lunch, but Mr Bluett asked me what it has been costing me for lunches. I said about 9d a day and so I don't know how much I will get although I will make on it anyway as I have been taking sandwiches with me.

Lately there has been a growing tendency for wardens volunteering as Shelter Marshall on Southwark Street Shelter. Tonight I have seen "the reason". She can play an accordeon quite good but that isn't the attraction. Tomorrow I will volunteer as Shelter Marshall but I am rather a late starter. I will have to get Pop to clean up the buttons on my uniform and I will have to repaint my "Anderson shelter".

Post 5 had some business last week. 2 HE bombs and a fire all together. The small "Laystalls" in Suffolk Street had the fire and the Stationery office copped the HE. Pocock Railway Bridge caught the other one. There is only one pair of lines left. The rest of the bridge adorns Pocock Street.

I am going to turn in now so cheerio, Love from Tom."

Tom had never seen his 16th birthday.

During the nights at home, I had the opportunity of hearing London's all night AA barrage. The family, having seen so much bombing (for being on the river, Southwark was one of the heavily bombed districts) would leave at night for Waterloo Station Shelter where they had bunks. They tried hard to coax me to go too but air raids were a novelty to me and I could afford to sleep indoors. They had to go or they would forfeit their tickets for their bunks. Had I seen as much daily destruction as the people at home, I too might forsake a bed for a subway bunk. My nights' sleep at home was often broken by the thunder of the local guns and more than once I heard the whine, thud and the clattering of the falling bricks with that strange ensuing silence which told me that that was not a gun.

A 10 weeks course finishing with 4 weeks at Redford Barracks, Edinburgh, sees me a 2nd Year Classified Signaller, a life far less as heavy worked as a gunners.

December 1940 : DUNBAR

At Dunbar, the troop is manning 6 inch Naval guns as Coastal Defence against the threatened invasion. Here, we are seeing a real Scottish winter which freezes your nose and fingers and piles up snowdrifts along the roads 6 feet deep in as many minutes.

I am getting my first practical experience as a signaller for Capt Stewart, and myself (at the phone) are in an observation pill box on the coast waiting to observe the fire from the guns firing 3 miles away at Bour House.

The whine and splash of the shots are followed by the thud of the guns which sent them. So far, firing has been good. A fishing trawler is coming round Crag's Head and the guns are about to fire again. I pass down "Stop" (Fire code word meaning Stop Firing) – but too late for already 200 lbs of HE are distributing trajectories through the air.

Our next fire order was "Cease Fire". Those last 2 rounds had fallen sending up twin columns of water perilously near that boat.

Next morning the local paper told how a trawler, reported being unsuccessfully bombed by an unseen plane, whilst the trawler was hugging the coast. After dropping 2 bombs the plane, which could not be seen in the low skies, apparently made off.

March 1941 : I had made my 3rd unsuccessful attempt to leave the unit.

Last August, when London first started getting bombed while we, the Army, were in the peace and serenity of Scotland, I had filled up various sheets for a transfer to London's Ack Ack defences, my transfer application never got further than the Battery Office. Last December, I had read in the paper that the Army CO's cannot hold back soldiers wishing transfer to the RAF. Armed with this newspaper clipping, I took it with my transfer application to the Battery Office, but Major Gold told me the news that the 155 was on a stand by order to go East the following Spring, and the personnel cannot be altered in a regiment already posted for service abroad.

The following March, two weeks before sailing date, I found myself in Lochart Hospital with Tonsilitus, the first week my temperature was high enough to assure me of missing the boat. Then my temperature gradually fell lower.

Despite jumping from my warm bed (after lights out) dashing cold water down my back and standing in front of an electric fan, I just would not catch a chill. My temperature came lower – almost normal.

I confided in my pretty nurse and asked her to fake my temperatures in her book. She, beautiful traitress, reported me to our Army MO when he visited me.

After a frank talk between the MO and myself, I altered his accusation that I was funking service abroad, to a promise that I would not be discharged till the 21st. The Regiment sailed on the 19th.

I had missed the boat!

But on the 18th, one day before sailing, Lt Brocklehurst had me prematurely discharged as he wanted me as his Gun Position Operator. And on the 19th, not yet well enough to be allowed to carry my own kit, I climbed up the gangplank of HMT Strathmore.

Chapter Nine

AFRICA

On my 22nd birthday, the convoy pulled in at our 1st port of call, Freetown on the West Coast of Africa. Here, for 3 days, we threw pennies to copper coloured bullet headed bum boatmen, who unable to sell us their fruit (forbidden to us by Orders) would dive into the shark waters and come up a minute later clutching the coins we had thrown in. And what a perfect Billingsgate language they hurled back at us, when, back on the surface after bursting their lungs in their submarine chase for that shilling, discover it is only a halfpenny in silver paper. All that glitters isn't silver. I'll wager that these negros had never learnt their English at the village church missionary school.

After 3 days, in which we sweltered on the decks by day, and in the cool nights, crowded the deck-rails watching the chain of native's fires, our convoy of 32 troopships once more pulled anchors and away.

April 1941 : CAPE TOWN

Wednesday 16th – Saturday 19th
On the first night that we swarmed into Cape Town, how welcome was the street lighting and flashing neon signs, after 2 years of blackouts. Had it not been for the lighting,

we would not have noticed the charming and shapely coloured girls in their fashionable European clothes. But in our 4 short days ashore, we discovered the "colour bar" – it just wasn't done to be seen mixing with the coloured people.

The male blacks do the labour, the Dutchmen of the town drive the buses whilst their daughters serve as shop salesgirls, and the British do the administrative side. Outside the town are the farmsteads of the Dutch and British settlers with bad feeling gradually building up between them.

Yet how these Sunny South Africans opened up their heart and homes to help make our short stay one of our happiest memories. In these 4 days, never once did Doug Brewer and myself have a dull moment. No sooner did we tire of walking the town admiring the semi-sky scrapers (the Post Office and Shell Mex) than we would accept one of the invites that the Cape Townies were always sending into the Army canteens. Then away for a car trip round the town, the seafront or the inland farmsteads and finishing up with dinner or tea at our hostess's home.

On one of these trips, I had the enjoyable experience of seeing the lights of Cape Town and the bay from the motor road which climbs almost half way up the Table Mountain.

The last day, when Doug and myself were having a bus trip to the end of its route (bus services being free to us), our bags of grapes in our laps caused a joke, a conversation and of course the inevitable invitation home with an old Scottish fruit farmer hailed from his Scotland home for the past 42 years. His Surrey-born wife gave us a royal welcome. They had been South African long enough to adopt that strange nasal twang of the Colonial.

They had us "setting de-own" to their table for 3 meals during our visit. And how we demolished the pile of roast lamb, sweet potatoes and buttered mealies at dinner.

Sitting in their armchairs in front of a fake fireplace (it is always too sunny for fires), chatting like old friends and listening in to London for the wireless news made it all seem like a night at home. And when it was time for us to leave for the docks, they even insisted on paying our 2 shilling train fare !

Chapter Ten

INDIA

5th May 1941 : INDIA

Old soldiers say "the best view of India is Bombay when seen from the rear end of the boat". But I hardly think that a just criticism as we watch the slowly approaching sea of tall white buildings, golden domes and pointed steeples of Bombay. The "Strathmore" slides alongside Bombay docks. From the elevated position of the decks, we hold a fine view of the wide sun glaring roads and tall European commercial buildings. Along the dockside, groups of half naked Indian children do acrobatics and deformed kiddies exhibit their elephantitus legs or limbless stumps with exaggerated looks of self pity. Now and again they bleat a chorus of "Backsheesh Sahibs".

We see little more of Bombay for no sooner are we off the boat than we are piling into the brown Military train bound for Ahmednagar.

India – The Gem of the Empire. The school text book that taught me that, never described these Indian villages we are passing through - Native men, their many wives, children, cattle and fowls all living in corrugated iron hovels with cow dung roofs. Yet how gracefully the women and girls carry themselves with their brass pots balanced on their heads. The hard caked countryside slipping past the windows is barren and dusty, the river beds and water ways dry, their beds baked hard. The train frightens crowds of monkeys as we cut through rocky country.

At Poona, we have a halt for some tea and sandwiches and welcome they are too. Dusk will shortly be due so we roll down shirt sleeves and drop the turn-ups of our shorts to fall as slacks – as added anti-malaria precautions, we smear anti-mosquito cream over our hands, faces and necks. Bdr Robson, who has already soldiered here in past years, says the mozzies thrive on that cream. The stuff soon makes us sweat especially as our carriage windows are all closed to stop thieving fingers as well as mosquitos from entering. In each compartment is an electric fan. Some awkward beggar - further along the coach - has already put his hand into the revolving blades and they are unearthing the First Aid box. Most of the chaps have already bedded down on the folding bed racks but as I have clicked for the train guard, I haven't bothered about my bed.

By 3am the train has reached "Naggar". Indian SC trucks are already waiting to transport us to Artillery Barracks. Every tree along the road is whistling – there must be hundreds of crickets on the leaves. The stone barracks don't look very inviting in the darkness, nothing is ready for our reception so we bed down on the stone floors of a bungalow and pass the remaining couple of hours darkness sleeping soundly despite the insects which are sucking our rich thick blighty blood. Maybe as we get acclimatised and our blood runs thinner, the insects won't be so anxious to use our hands and arms for 7 course dinners.

June 1941 – AHMEDNAGAR, DECCAN

We are now settled down to Indian soldiering – it isn't a very strenuous life. Reveille comes at 6.30 and morning parades finish before the sandy parade grounds start simmering in the midday head of 107°. Afternoon parades from 4.30 to 6.30 finish up a leisurely working day to 5 total hours. We pass the siesta period from 2-4.30 on the bed sheets with our mosquito nets draped round our beds looking like so many sleeping princesses. Every gust of wind blows a blast of hot air through the open barrack doors but the groaning punkah frames swinging above our beds keep the billet reasonably cool.

It's a lazy life. Just call "Boy" and white haired Kishan comes gliding in and does his bidding to make your bed, clean your boots or scrub your equipment. With each one of 12 of us paying him 8 annas a week, he is a well paid worker. He works round the billet for 12 hours a day before he leaves for his home 5 miles across the fields. These are pretty old barracks. They recently housed some of the thousands of Italian prisoners that Wavell took in Libya – their names are still on our kit boxes.

The first morning here, most of us lost our breakfast. Dining facilities were not yet organised for us and we just drew our breakfast from the cookhouse and made for the billets to eat it. Only Innocents and Fools would have done that. Walking across the Square with my filled plate and mug, I had hardly gone 15 yards when a shadow fell across my plate, something dropped like a stone and there I was, watching a Sky Hawk 50ft high with my breakfast dangling in it's claws.

I joined the group of earlier victims on the veranda, ready

to laugh at the expense of the next man to lose his grub, the same as they had laughed at me.

We are wise to the Mohammedan char wallahs, fruit wallahs, tonga wallahs and bazaar wallahs. They, all of them, must have made a harvest out of us before we understood the currency, and before we learnt that a third of the money is counterfeit. It took 3 days before I discovered 16 annas make 1 Rupee. The fruit wallah had been giving me change at 14 annas to the Rupee. The 8 anna bit the char wallah gave me, I soon learn to be 'crab' (bad). So 'crab' is it that the tonga wallah immediately gave it back to me with a pained look when I tried to pass it to him in the dark as my tonga fare to the bazaar. Even in the bazaar, where kiddies pestered us with their choruses of 'No mudder, no farder, backsheesh sahib', I gave it to one little villain who soon came back pulling my elbow (and my attention) to his 'crab' 8 annas.

The fruit wallah had been allowing us credit against our names till pay day, but the annas marked against our names grew quicker than the credit purchases we made. We soon discovered his trick of putting odd annas against our names in his spare time.

However, a few 'nom de plumes' soon altered his short cut to fortune. The next week, Johnny fruit wallah was running from billet to billet trying to collect his money for bananas marked against such names as 'Charlie Chaplin', 'Adolph Stalin' and 'Cowboy Charlie', and it took some time before he learnt that although 'Annie Lawrie' had got 14 annas worth of bananas against her name, now that it was time to collect the money it appeared 'Little Annie doesn't live here any more'. Some of the chaps are already letting the lattocist daub snakes on their arms and chest, and for 7 annas a week the nappy will shave you while you sleep at 4 o'clock in the morning.

The most welcome visitor to the cantonment is the snake charmer. After stupefying cobras with his flute, he lets a mongoose fight and kill one of his snakes. But ever since the lads all vanished after the show before he could collect his money, he always insists he gets his money from the troops, 'in anticipation' – before the show.

I went down with Jock to the bazaar. The same old routine, as we pass along the smelly streets, - hawk-nose salesmen with oily smiles enticing us into their shops, offering bargains in cameras, knifes, shirts etc. Once in a shop we picked up a padlock. 'Kitna?' (how much). 'To you Sahib, 12 annas'. Then a long haggling argument until the price drops to a reasonable price of 6 annas. We are buying a real Indian silk shirt as well so he lets us have the padlock for 4 annas.

Once more in the street I notice Jock's toupee doesn't fit him so well – it is almost a juggling act the way he balances it on his head. The reason? He takes off his toupee and inside it's crown is a singlet he 'lifted' from the counter when the man's back was turned.

That singlet only completes an otherwise bad bargain. The real Indian silk shirt is tabbed 'Made in Japan', and the key snaps in the padlock.

Give me London where goods are displayed and priced and shopping is a pleasure instead of a haggling bout.

14 June 1941: Six of us, all signallers, are going north on a 3-day's rail journey of 3,500 miles to Kohat on the NW

Frontier. We are off for a month's course on RAF Co-operation. It comes as a shock to discover we are expected to buy our own food for the next 3 days from our last pay day's money. I have to allow myself 24 annas a day for food and drink and with 2 poached eggs and toast costing 14 annas, it doesn't look as if I'll be too well fed this journey.

On the 2nd day's run, we start leaving the plains for the rugged hills of the north. Travelling first class is very convenient – our compartment is like a small room with 6 leather bunk beds and toilet room. The natives travel 3rd class and the stench from their crowded coaches hangs in the nostrils long after the coach has passed. At the crowded stations, it amuses me the numbers of people that still come tumbling from the coaches long after enough have already poured out to have filled the coach 3 times over. Yet still they flood out, Hindus with their flowing sheets entangling their legs, Mohammedans in their billowy white cotton trousers, women carrying enormous bundles and trailing children by the litter. These stations are a hubbub of colour and noise. Bearded Sikhs in their coloured turbans always seem to stand aside with their womenfolk from the crowds. Sikh women are lovely to look at but even so do not equal the Parsee girls who are strangely enough as white as Europeans. As the train enters each station, we are besieged by the porter coolies anxious to earn annas for carrying. No sooner do they see we are not leaving the train, then off in a pack to the next likely customers. Water carriers (Bhistes) bring their water (panee) for the different castes, Moslims, Mohammedans, Hindus, etc, and refreshment caterers slap up queer chapattis and maize cakes over hot plates and sell betel nut and melon seeds to the native travellers.

Betel is popular, they chew it well until their lips become blood red and spit the red juice over the platform. As we pass Agra, near Delhi, low mist robs me of seeing the famous Taj Mahal. Along the line, we pass the Ghats, burial pyres of sticks supporting corpses ready for burning whilst buzzards and naked neck vultures sit around waiting to take their part in the finale of the burial service. New Delhi is well lit up as we pass it in the night. I would like to visit New Delhi. We pass Lahore and change at Rawalpindi for the final day's journey.

The countryside slipping past is hilly, rugged and desolate. After a further 24 hours travel with hardly seeing a village among the hills, we finally pile our kit onto the deserted Kohat station platform 8 o'clock on Sunday morning. Not knowing exactly where to go, we leave our baggage and make our way to some Royal Corps of Signals barracked 20 minutes walk from the station. Tall bearded hillmen, easily 6 feet high hang around the station steps – they seem quite defiant compared to the servile natives of the plains. Coffee, poast toasties, sausages, chips and green peas. How I enjoyed the breakfast the Signals gave us after the 5 frugal meals of eggs I had had in the past 3 days. After that, the Signals lent us their truck to transport us to No 28 Squadron RAF.

July 1941 : KOHAT

The past month's course has been well spent – the RAF live like Lords. The aerodrome bungalows are pleasantly situated among well laid out lawns with wireless extensions onto the lawns and tennis courts and swimming pools. The food has been superb, eating has been a pleasure. The whole camp is wired off and patrolled by Indian Infantry. This is in the hostile area and it's forbidden to go out alone or unarmed. Air raid sirens stand ready as alarms for a tribesmen attack, but the last trouble was 2 years ago. The weather is much hotter than Ahmednagar - 113°F daily.

Our working day finishes at 1pm for the morse would soon send us to sleep in the heat. About 20 artillery signallers, 6 from 5th, 6 from 155th and the remainder from Indian Artillery regiments, have been tutored by an Australian RAF Signals Officer on Air Shoots, and speeding up our morse from the RA 10 words / min to the RAF 25 word / min. The RA Signallers will shortly replace RAF Ground Signallers in Air Co-operation. The second week, we have been putting our knowledge into practice stuck up in a dummy cockpit over a model range. The past couple of weeks we have had actual air shoots with the RAF planes in W/T communication with the ground. I have been one of the privileged 6 to go up in the rear cockpit for 5 shoots lasting ½ of an hour. I found it not so exciting as I expected for once up in the air, you experience no feeling of rushing through the air but only feel suspended in mid-air, only looking over the side at the circling ribbons that are roads and the cotton wool puffs that are the detonations you are observing, do you realise you are moving. The most unpleasant experience is the banking and climbing when the horizon swings through the quarter circle from horizontal to vertical and your belly falls first to your boots before rebounding to your chest. I was relieved to see the tarmac rushing up to meet our landing wheels again. I am afraid I hadn't been much use to the pilot as observer but I doubt he expected me to be.

The 3 days return journey lengthened to 4. The monsoons had been falling in the plains and the railway lines had been swept away by flood and landslides. For 46 weeks in 52, India lies dusty, cracked and parched. The monsoons bring rains strong enough to sweep aside villages, bridges and railways. How or why they cannot conserve the surplus water as reservoirs for the rest of the year when good soil becomes dust through drought, I cannot fathom. The 24 hours delay through floods caused us to be at Delhi the day we should have arrived at Poona - our destination. And of course, broke with our money expired at Delhi too with 1,000 miles yet to go.

Ramsay and myself filled in a couple of hungry hours walking the scorched streets through Delhi. With nothing in our pockets, we felt like joining the naked beggars begging backsheesh. Camels pulling carts, homeless wretches sleeping in the park, and a magnificent building 'The Bank of India', standing in a road of ramshackled buildings – this is my impression of Delhi. To make matters worse, when our train came in that night, we got in the end coach and awoke next morning to find our coach (and us) deserted and standing alone on a railway shunting siding. We got our kit portered to the nearest station by coolies and managed to muster up a few annas among us for paying them – but the small amount caused them to give us some very black looks (if such is possible from a black man).

We were desperately hungry so we had a good meal in the station refreshment rooms and paid with a chitty of our names and regiment. After all, we felt our plight due to the cockeyed arrangement of the Regiment sending us 3,500 miles each way without ration money, I hope when the refreshment room manager applied to our CO for a refund that he made on the deal. At 11 at night we reached our barracks at Kirkee (the Regiment having moved during our absence) and I was glad to turn in.

Next morning when we expected an apology from the office for the trouble we had been caused by the Regiment not sending us transport to meet us at Poona station, (we had to get the RTO to hire us a taxi), and for sending us on a 6 days journey without ration money – we got instead 2 drubbings down.

Firstly – Why did you not report to the Regimental Office on your arrival. And that at 11 at night in a barracks where you had never seen your own barrack room let alone run around in the dark looking for the Regimental Office.

Secondly – Explain how you are 32 hours late. And the whole railway system dislocated by floods !! What a life !

We have just had a 3 days pukkha divisional drill order with Punjabe and Sikh infantry co-operating, making advances under live barrage that we put down for them. The RAF also helped us out by dropping flour bombs on us. One bomb which caught us on the road fell between Carr and myself splattering Carr with flour. He hopes it's not an omen.

We have now got Australian technical equipment, American transport and 4.5 inch howitzers. Everything points to us leaving India shortly. Kirkee is usually the stepping off place from India. 25 pounders go West (Egypt) and 4.5s usually go East. If that rule holds good we will shortly be sailing towards the Rising Sun.

I have had a week's driving instruction under young Sandy Johnson. I would like to have a proper driving course for signallers, should be classified drivers anyway. However thanks to Sandy, I have learnt to drive his 15 cwt Chevrolet – all I want now is experience. He took me along Poona Road on a trial run. He could not have picked a worse road. Swaying bullock carts, goats, chickens, plenty of natives with their loads on their heads, how I got along without hitting anything I don't know. When we reached the crossroads where the point duty native policeman flings his arms about like a windmill, directing traffic, I was made to drive straight across. Halfway over, Sandy said 'Turn right'. I did and nearly took the dusky traffic cop for a ride on our bonnet. He saved himself by the nimblest bit of sidestepping I've ever seen. He almost turned white with fright.

However, as I've said before – all I need is experience.

Chapter Eleven

AT SEA

28 August 1941 : MALACCA STRAITS

I sailed for France in a pleasure steamer. It was crowded though comfortable. I sailed for India in a 20,000 tons luxury liner – it was crowded but comfortable.

For the past 10 days we have been tossing about en route for Malaya in the dirtiest scruffiest tub (3,000 tons) ploughing the seas. We are crowded but far from comfortable. We have had 100 men picketed on fire guard at different points in the boat every night and with only 280 men available for guards, it means a guard almost every other night. This old coffin ship used to be a cattle boat before they decided to make it a transport. The old tub pitches and tosses taking our stomachs with it on its every lurch. Only 5 of the sentry posts are up on deck. The rest are below deck on the crowded troop quarters, round the thumping stinking engine room or worse of all, around the galleys. Nobody, not even the sailors among us can stand for 2 hours at a time, with a life jacket muffling the chest and trying to stand on a swaying deck and at the same time breathe in lungfulls of odours of engine oil, lascars quarters, curry and bilge.

We were all sick, horribly sick, the kind which turns your

face green and makes you feel death itself the only relief. The whole crew, the galley staff included, are black lascars. They prepare our food in the dirtiest fashion and even before its preparation, the meat is mildewed and the bread flour has weevils. The cooked food, when it reaches our mess table, stays on it just long enough to enable us to open up the port flaps before throwing it out to poison any sharks foolish enough to be following this boat. Fortunately, seasickness takes away our appetite. My diet has been chocolate biscuits and tea which I buy from the Regimental Canteen. The name of the crate is the Ekma. When we refer to it we always twist the name to Altmark after the German Prison ship recently intercepted by the Navy off Norway. The prisoners were saved before they finished their passage.

Our salvation will be the finish of the journey itself. It should not be long now before we are on terra firma. The more firmer, less terror.

3 September 1941 : We should be docking in Port Swettenham in an hour's time. I've been wearing this shirt an hour and done nothing more strenuous than lean over the deck rail, yet my shirt is sodden in sweat. This is a clammy moist heat. India was hotter yet dry. The jungle comes right down to the yellow muddy water's edge. I can't imagine artillery being any use here if all Malaya is as overgrown as this.

6 September 1941 : The night before last we arrived in this wooden bungalow camp in the middle of acres of rubber trees. The Aussies transported us from Ipoh station for our guns and vehicles will come on by road. In the 180 miles rail journey from the docks I have only seen Chinese, although I did see a few Malayan houses standing on their stilts among the swampy country. Apparently, this is the rainy season – and can it rain! It falls in sheets. No wonder the camp is threaded with 5ft deep drainage ditches. The heavy foliage makes the place pitch black at night and it's only when you step into space and your chin hits the ground that you know you stepped down one of these ditches. Each morning the Chinese women rubber tree tappers wearing black cotton trousers, and some of their kiddies, come round tapping the rubber from the trees.

The past two nights we have wandered over to the nearby Aussie camp where they made us royally welcome to their canteen. But now regimental orders forbid us going there. British Officers never have liked the Australians' lax discipline, doubtless, they are afraid we will get into the Aussie's free and easy style if we mix with them. They are a big husky crowd and a fine lot at that. As one of them said to our Colonel who had checked him for not giving a salute – "Look here brother" said the Aussie "We are free and easy. We don't salute our own officers so I'm damned if I'm saluting you". Was our Old Man mortified!

9 September 1941 : IPOH

Ipoh Town is out of bounds. However last night, Will and myself strolled to the Aussie camp where they gave us a lift into town. After a walk round, we hailed a rickshaw outside the Ruby Cinema and told him to take us to the YMCA. The rickshaw puller took us for a 25 minutes tour and it was only after recognising shops and places for the second time of passing that we saw through his game. We paid him what he deserved and sought directions to the YMCA. It was then we discovered the YMCA to be only 150 yards from the Ruby. 25 minutes for 150 yards.

The YMCA is run by British, American and Dutch civilians,

mostly planters. The teas, suppers, salads, drinks and ice cream are delicious, as well as cheap. We'll be here quite a lot, for a radiogram, billiards and table tennis are only a few of the pastimes they had to offer us.

We passed an hour in the Jubilee dancehall watching the dancing. Dancing is run on the American taxi style. A dollar ticket lets you onto the floor for 3 dances with one of the hostesses. The hostesses are mostly Chinese girls, a few Malayans, all looking glamorous in their oriental dance dresses cut on Western styles. But the girls have too short a stride to dance good Western ballroom dances.

Outside the Chinese cinema, a well spoken Chinese offered to drive us round the town until his wife left the cinema. He was the Chief Police Superintendent. The saluting policemen we drove past supported this. He showed us a secret - some Japanese shops had luminous painted roofs. These would point out a compass direction for Jap night bombers should war come. He assured us the police would act quickly on that day.

Novembe 1941 : KEDAH STATE

Sungai Patani – Those '101' sets are useless in this wooded country – the trees reduce wireless communication to a couple of hundred yards. Normal range is 5-10 miles. Major Gold was so concerned over this that he sent the 6 battery wireless cars and their signallers on a 4 days journey round Malaya – testing the wireless under different country conditions. What a time we had. Communications on the move were perfect, but considering that the first and last trucks were barely a mile apart, it hardly proved anything. However, in four days we covered a lot of Malaya, seeing the beautiful Cameron Highlands, the tin mining States and a town like Kuala Lumpur. We bivouacked nightly outside a town so as to pop in for a few hours pleasure. Lt Brocklehurst was the only Officer and so we were a happy party.

Somewhere in Malaya

Now, most of the chaps are north, at Jittra, a few miles south of the jungles bordering Thailand. They are preparing a gun position against a Japanese invasion. Thanks to Tropical Ringworm on my chest (a parasite from the rubber trees) and Dhobi Itoh caused by damp, I will be unable to join them till later.

Jittra – Surrey Camp. Am having an enjoyable 10 days helping to build a troop command post in the guise of a Malayan house. The gun trenches must be built up for the ground here is flat and wet. This State is one of the rice growing States and were we to dig below ground level, the water from the surrounding padi fields would rapidly drain into the trenches. Plenty of snakes here – have so far killed one a day. At the Surrey Camp, they shot a python asleep in the padre's armchair! Have been on one expedition north, cutting bamboo from the jungle. Never again. It is depressing in the dark in the jungle, and a blow with your axe fetches down a shower of red ants three quarters of an inch long from the leaves. They nearly drive you mad with their bites. The Chinese kiddies sell us freshly cut pineapples at 10 cents each. My lips are acid raw with eating them. To think the pineapples at home cost 10 times as much.

8 December 1941 : Since the war, newspaper medical columns have all recommended the value of a cup of tea in times of stress and excitement. Yet yesterday, my most exciting day found me repeatedly deprived of this restorative. Nippon pulled our noses when she bombed Sungai Patani Aerodrome a mile or so from where we were, with her 'insignificant and 3rd rate airforce' before we hardly realised we were at war with them.

We sweated digging trenches and dispersing our guns'

ammunition and trucks for we might easily be next on their target list.

Teatime was just due when GE got immediate moving orders. Thinking of that hot tea which I would not have time for, I piled into GE just as it moved off. We would be moving off to Jittra 5 hours ahead of the rest of the battery. The guns would come up under cover of darkness.

Dusk found us in the maze of tracks, trucks and rubber trees of the Surrey Lines, while Captain Coles, our OP Officer, and Lt Eustace, our GPO went on ahead, we hastily unearthed our primus and pumped steadily until we had some water boiling. Just as it was bubbling, Eustace came back with orders to move. Once more we were cheated of our tea.

Later, when we were settled in our Troop Command Post, the wireless set erected, lines laid and exchange working, we had the tea dixie brewing again. A couple of maintenance signallers were hanging on, trying to find work enough to detain them in the Command Post until tea was ready. Captain Coles, after his muddy and tiring journey from his OP was also invited to join the expectant. At last, the tea was ready for sweetening. I went to the two tobacco tins, one of which I knew contained sugar. I whipped off its lid and sprinkled its white contents into the tea. A warning shout from Eustace came too late. A beautiful smell of washing day at home came up from the dixie and small bubbles started appearing. "Hell" declared Eustace. "I distinctly warned you not to take the soap flakes tin" Once more we had been robbed of our tea. Yet no – we were not going to be cheated of our tea a third time. We dipped our mugs and drank deep - straining the bubbles with our teeth! Meanwhile the Japs are 18 miles away.

13 December 1941 : What a crowded past 3 days. The first position was the low flying Jap plane which dropped leaflets over us. The Surreys, Leicesters and Gurkhas were busy with the enemy 18 miles away. Our only concern was the Malayans intent on betraying us. First we discovered the goalposts of the football field in front us, cut down and pointing arrow fashion to the Malayan houses concealing our guns. Then they drove cattle across the long padi to make conspicuous tracks from the air. A tree was mysteriously felled across the road and our telephone lines bared and short circuited. Our maintenance signallers caught a couple of bogus Malayan police sniping. Their suspicions were aroused because Jittra Police were all evacuated to Alor Star. The second position we moved into saw our first engagement of Japs arriving in buses. Poor Nobby Hall became our first fatal casualty in this affair and Reggie Spooner went back with a nasty gash right through his right chest. Benny Carson, slightly wounded, followed him. Major Gold sent down a rosy picture of the havoc we had caused and the last orders I put on my message pad was "Prepare to Advance". Yet the Punjabis trickling back through our position looked worn out and hungry. They hardly bore out any hopes of advancing. When we hurriedly struck our position back in the Surrey lines, it was with the knowledge that the Japs were just down the road. The Surreys (our front line) were digging in alongside us. What had happened I don't know. I hurriedly rigged up my wireless and tried to get in touch with our OP but no answers came back to my calls or to my morse. Our line signallers could not run a telephone line out with the Japs in between and so without an OP we just sat and waited. Everyone was touchy, the Japs could be anywhere and this silence didn't improve things.

Driver Notley, in the woods behind us saw a large white

Dhobi umbrella among the trees and gave a Parachutists alarm. Tuck looked at me and said "Goodbye pal, this is our lot". Two of our guns swung round to engage any enemy in our rear while the other two stood ready to the front. When the False Alarm had been realised, I decided to start doing something. Anything was better than sending unanswered calls out on the ether. So I packed up my set into GE and went to Sgt Robson's gun – he being shorthanded on account of his 3 casualties. My gunners' training came in handy, for we were joined by an infantryman - the last of his surrounded forward platoon, who had swum a lake on his way back to us. Eustace decided to shell the road a bit and gave a range 2000 yards. "2000 yards" exclaimed our comrade "they were a bloody sight nearer than that when I left them". We had hardly fired our first round when the whole of our immediate front became a firework display of tracer bullets shooting toward us. Our bren opened up and there in the waist high padi, 200 yards in front of us suddenly came the first line of Jap infantry. If the guns were to be saved it was only by independent limber up. "He who fights and runs away, lives to fight another day". I stayed to help limber up before running to the shack behind which GE would be waiting for me. But all I found was it's tyre tracks. GE had fled ! I ran back and just managed to clamber onto a moving gun quad. At Alor Star Aerodrome (already bombed to uselessness), we took up section positions firing in the darkness onto the road to hold up the break through. We had lost 2 quads and 2 limbers in that last scramble. I was pleased to see my pal Will turn up on a motorbike. He had had a busy minute trying to kick over it's engine with bullets spluttering about him. He was dog tired after a long and tiring day. I was very sorry, when 6 hours later, I helped lift him into the ambulance at Guron. He had fallen asleep when driving in our convoy and had piled his bike on top of himself. Injuries including a fractured kneecap would keep him out of the War for a time. I would miss him.

16 December 1941 : Guron – KEDAH PEAK
4 o'clock in the morning and as we have no OP, wireless is off the air and I am taking my turn with the line signallers manning the telephone exchange. Our four guns on the crest of the hill are silent, the gunners snatching a couple of hours rest in between sentry tours. We are in a funny position here in that we have no line of infantry in front of us.

Yesterday, we saw the infantry we should be covering, marching past in file, on file either side of the road. They were the 2/2nd Gurkhas – poor beggars they looked well spent. Little wonder considering they have had 4 days in the line without food. Nobody seems too comfortable in this position. Lt Eustace sampled his whisky last night – a sure sign he doesn't like the position either. Immediately behind us is the mountain of Kedah Peak. Since 3 o'clock this morning, I've been listening to the chatter of Tommy and bren guns. I ventured to phone Black at the Battery CP asking him what he made of it. He says the Sikhs are making an attack. Yet this hardly explains away machine gunfire coming from our rear! In the meantime we appear to be the only troops around here. We have seen none of the usual columns coming and going. Even the civilians all fled this peak days ago.

19 December 1941 : Once more we've done it – just got out by the skin of our teeth. Just as I had suspected, those machine guns were the Japanese Infantry behind us. We have escaped encirclement but Brigade HQ behind us has been surrounded and taken prisoners. We've had some bombing especially when we took up an exposed position on a football pitch. Little wonder passing bombers stopped to pay their compliments to four howitzers and a wireless truck stuck in the middle of a playing field. Half the time we are dealing with Japs in front of us – the other half dealing with them behind us !

23 December 1941 : PERAK STATE

Once more we are in our pre-invasion camp among the rubber trees, but under somewhat different conditions. 'B' battery is getting re-equipped with 25 pounders but we are hanging on to our howitzers. We are behind the line but meanwhile the fighting is keeping the troops busy north of here. We are only one division (11th) with nothing in reserve of us. The other division (9th) is similarly placed up on the other front on the East side of Malaya. The 9th and 11th complete the British Army in the field. There is an Australian division on the Muor River, south of here in Johore but apparently the Aussies are being held to their Prime Minister's statement made after the Crete disaster when he said that never again would the Aussies go into action without Air Support. Until that air support is forthcoming, the 9th and 11th can hold the 'thin red line'. The Japs are bombing our airfields before our planes have had a chance to take off. Johnny Jap has an advantage over us in his tanks, planes, navy and plenty of infantry. We have not one of these four things. We might have had a navy had the Singapore Times not printed the news that our latest battleship "The Prince of Wales" and the "Repulse" were coming to these waters to replace "HMAS Sydney" recently sunk. But now both battleships are on the bottom with the "Sydney" – thanks to a faked message which drew them out to meet an imaginary invasion convoy. Instead they met a reception committee of a fleet of Japanese torpedo bomber planes. Our ships, needless to say, had no air support and once more Air Power crippled Sea Power. The Navy, stout lads, put up a good show against the bombers but no battleship will float with 15 torpedos in it's side.

We the Army, are now feeling the pinch for we have little infantry, certainly not enough to deal with the Japanese invasion forces constantly coming down the undefended coastline and landing in the rear of the front line troops.

Our infantry have had it hard. The Gurkhas have been cut off and cut up time and again. They make an attack and find no enemy to engage. Then suddenly they are surprised and cut up by a shower of bullets issuing from the tree tops above their heads. The Japanese Guerrilla troops have been climbing high up among the tree tops and have been playing a 'hide and seek' war with them doing the hiding and us taking it. The Surreys and the Leicesters have lost many men and the remainder of both have been amalgamated to form the BB – British Battalion.

Chapter Twelve

XMAS DAY IN HAPPY VALLEY

25 December 1941 : KAMPAR VALLEY

Xmas Day in Happy Valley and we are sitting pretty. Our guns are well dug in and concealed, and command a field of fire at the opening of the valley. Either side of us the hills sweep up as a good protection against low flying aircraft. We have had a couple of planes round us but the heavy formations have been passing right over bound for Singapore. The Gurkhas are digging in small detachments along the valley and either side in the hills. Our OP is up in the hills too and commands a fine view of the valley. We should hold this place for long enough. The road through the valley is on the curve of the letter D. As long as they do not advance down the main road, that is to say the main stroke of the D, and thus cut us off, we should make a good stand. I had a long climb with Limb (my brother signaller) up the hillside to help prepare an alternative OP and on the way, we stopped to look in at an abandoned shack. We found a young dog, pot bellied with starvation, since it was left some days ago, so we dropped it in a weighted sack into a deep waterhole. I had a fright when a thunder of hoofs and a crashing of undergrowth heralded something breaking through the bush at me. It proved to be a wild pig but a hurriedly thrown brick diverted it. The Gurkhas are killing idle moments by using their crooked knives to throw and pin the chickens to the ground at 25 yards range. We have had a little excitement. Once when a Japanese patrol led by a German officer came down over the hills to pay us a visit. They came to stay – the German being the first to pack a bullet, the rest of the patrol being similarly received. The second alarm was when a tribe of large monkeys came bounding down the hillside, thumping and screaming. Somebody must have disturbed them from their homes in the hilltops. We have been on the alert but nobody has shown himself.

27 December 1941 : At 11 o'clock daily, I test wireless communications to the Wagon Lines 15 miles away to our rear. The Wagon Line set, operated by Jolliffe, is in RE, whilst my own set remains in the truck GE. I have however erected 90 feet of copper wire as a Wyndham Aerial between the trees so I should get better reception. So far I have barely been able to pick out Jolliffe's thin piping morse for it has been practically drowned in the flood of strong morse from friend and foe and the crash and crackling of atmospherics which forever fill my headphones. This morning, I stoop beneath the netting and sprigs, which try to make the track look like a bush from the air, and climb into the truck and switch on my set. After setting the frequency, I switch to "send" and watch the ammeter needle swing over as I press my key, adjusting the anode taps and tuning dial until I get a maximum reading. Switching to "receive" I tune till my earphones feel alive and I am now ready for Jolliffe so I work my fingers on the key as the key clicks out my call.......

VE PMB. PMB V PMC. PMC. AR.

I recognise his steady answer among the deluge of morse coming in and a little fine adjustment brings his answer in.......

VE PMC. PMC V PMB PMB. R7. AR.

I too can hear him R7 (meaning 'good'). With R7 on key we might even be clear on speech. I suggest this to him by sending him VE PMB V PMC Try R/T AR. He acknowledges and what a surprise when I switch to "receive / speech" and hear his sing song Liverpudlian voice in my earphones chanting "Hello Colo, Bolo Calling. Report my signals, Bolo to Colo Over". I've never had such clear reception and am glad I had put up the new aerial. It had been put up in the daily torrential downpour and I had sent my soul to hell with my curses at the trouble but it was apparently worth it. Sgt Mitchell I/C Signals put his head in the truck with his usual question "How's things". "Not bad at all" I answer. "I'm getting him Strength Seven Speech. How's that for 15 miles away". I finish up fishing for congratulations. "15 miles away damn all" he answers. "If that's RE you are talking to, it's coming up here now". Surprised I look out just as RE turns in off the road onto the gun position. Here is RE coming up following the muddy track between the trees with its 9 feet of brass aerial sticking up from the side and bashing against the lower branches of the trees as it jolts along beneath them. I can hear Jolliffe's voice this time without earphones. "Hello Colo, hear you strength niner" and out pops his head to poke fun at our wireless triumph.

Disgusted I move my frequency dial a fraction and listen to the short wave programme from Penang recently captured by the Japs. The Jap commentator speaking in his over modulated English is telling us – "...and so, my English friends, you are letting the native troops do the dirty fighting whilst you sit back. Similarly, you only evacuated the British from Penang, and the Chinese who looked to you for protection were left behind. But just as our bombers destroyed your flagship 'The Prince of Wales' so shall they seek out and destroy you. Goodbye my friends and have a Happy New Year – those of you who will live to see it".

Today's battery orders which have just come in by DR from the Wagon Lines states "All Ranks will scrub their webbing equipment, belts, haversack and pack. Troop Commanders will ensure that this is done".

Meanwhile the War carries on.

The Scheme of Things said we were to hold Kampar Valley for 2 weeks. We have done so and spent the last 4 or 5 days firing on many varied targets at all hours of the day or night. Our targets ranged from a trench mortar and it's crew, later it's burial party and a bridge over which Jap armoured cars were about to pass. Of course, bridge blowing is the Royal Engineers pigeon, but when they pulled the plunger, the bridge refused to go up as a roaring column of dust and falling masonry, for the simple reason that the REs had forgotten to put in a charge. As the oncoming cars did not seem likely to hang around until the error was rectified, the 155 were hurriedly called in to plaster HE on the bridge instead. The night we left the valley was dark and wet, the leaves dripping steadily long after the rain had ceased. I was detailed by Eustace to remain behind to join the joint OP Infantry line to the CP line, and I would be picked up by a signal truck a couple of hours later. I passed a miserable two hours in the dark and damp trench waiting. I did wander around a bit, but as this was to be the new formed infantry front line it wasn't too healthy. For when Johnny Gurkha challenges you, the first intimation that you have discovered a sentry is when a bayonet shoots out and stops just short of your Adam's apple. It is then that he asks for the password. I never wandered around inviting too many challenges in case I should meet one who couldn't understand English.

30 December 1941 : CHANDIERANG

I have heard the New Year Celebrations from home. Limb and myself have been dumped with rifles and rations to man the telephone exchange in this deserted tin mine for the next 24 hours. We seemed right out of the war, no sound of gunfire and the only Jap plane that did fly over, we heard whining into a dive and crash. Next day when we rejoined the regiment 7 miles away, a B Battery bren gunner claimed credit for bringing it down. Otherwise everything was quiet and in 24 hours we only put through 5 calls (the line and exchange had been taken over by Divisional HQ). The only person we saw was an old Chinese woman who sold us pineapples. At some time around 11pm, we got a call from the Corps of Signals who wanted to know if we needed to hear some music to cheer us a while. They then tuned their wireless set into the London Overseas Programme putting their wireless earphones to their telephone mouthpiece and thus relayed to our earpieces – a good old programme of New Year songs and festivities. It was fine to hear Big Ben and wintry London speaking to us 12,000 miles away where New Year was being spent in 90°F with 250,000 men fighting for the other half of Malaya. The Japs the half they haven't got, and the British for the half they have lost.

The Jap planes, knowing there is practically no RAF opposition, are having a jolly time pot shot bombing trucks and machine gunning troops and roads.

Fortunately the roads either side are wooded and afford us welcome protection. No sooner do we take to the road then a plane, with engine off, swoops low over the trees alongside the road unseen by us and then swing out over us and open up. Things are so bad, each truck has it's own roof watcher to warn the driver. The planes work in patrols of 3. Each patrol covers it's own small area, bombing anything or anybody which shows itself. Every 20 minutes they get relieved by a new patrol of 3. The old planes do not leave the skies until their relief arrives. Thus our whole area is open to Jap eyes and guns - they having planes out from dawn to dusk. Twisted and burnt truck chassis litter the road at regular intervals – only light bombs hit them yet it is all that's required.

One of the nasty jobs I have been called on to do is to enter villages to help turn villagers out from their homes – no easy job. When we were north among the Malayans (who are like Japs both in looks and outlook) the job did not call for a hard heart for they were mostly hostile to us and pro-Japanese. But as we come south among the friendly Chinese and Tamils, it takes a lot to barge into a house and evict families from their homes. Yet it is in our interest they should be turned out of the war area for apart from any likely 5th columnists among them, the Japs would extort information from them were they to fall in Jap hands. So as we come south we drive the evacuees before us.

Chapter Thirteen

JANUARY 1942 – TANK ALERT

7 January 1942

A few events at Slim River, a mile behind the line. This side of the bridge is the Chinese village that seemed so important to Jap bombers yesterday. Now it is empty, shops stand open, their stocks open for all to take. In the wooded clump alongside the village, the six of us are digging a command post whilst the gun sergeants are selecting likely gun platforms among the trees. The batteries' howitzers, gunners and transport are in Wagon Lines 4 miles back. The guns aren't coming up till 3 this afternoon. Swinging a pick in this heat soon makes your shirt cling to your back. Considering our comfort before safety, we throw aside our tin hats, and peel off our shirts. Hardly have we done so when one of Nippon's planes, forever circling above, sees our white bodies among the trees contrasted against the dark shadows and leaves. Branches snap and fall from above us as the first bullets splatter through the treetops. Now we know as we pile into our half dug trench, that our gun position has already been betrayed to the enemy by our thoughtlessness. A known enemy gun position will soon be sorted out for attention.

The truck M2, detailed to bring us up our midday meal from the Wagon Lines, is long overdue. We fill the holes in our stomachs with biscuits and minerals taken 'ad lib' from the deserted village. At last, the position prepared to climb into GE and drive back to the battery. On the way we pass a truck, or rather it's remains, all twisted and smouldering black. The identity plate shows our regimental number and below that M2. We do not linger long for already the plane that blew our rations and M2 to hell is hovering like a vulture ready to send us after them.

The battery is moving into position. GE, our 15 cwt wireless truck, with Lt Eustace GFP, Charlie Levitt his ack, myself and Ray Limb hanging out with his neck craned up for he is 'watcher' for the bombers, leaves the friendly protection of the rubber trees in the Wagon Lines and bumps onto the road. We move off quickly partly because it's dangerous every minute on the road and partly because wireless, lines, gun zero lines etc, are best completed before the guns arrive. A bomb hole threatens to block the road so we pull up whilst Eustace calls to some Engineers to fill it in for the following guns. That halt probably saves our lives. We have been leading the convoy, but when we pull in, BSM Billings on his motorbike passes by giving us a 'thumbs up' salute. He is closely followed by a B Battery gun, with Bdr Bland riding on the gun as 'watcher'. They disappear around the bend. A little later, bursts of machine gun fire suggest a plane is letting them have an exciting time. But when we eventually move off, we are again halted by the sight of Bdr Bland, this time riding pillion on a motorbike, coming down the road waving us to stop. He soon makes himself clear. "Tanks broken through, Billings has got it. The gun and quad ran into them on the bridge". Bland being on the gun behind the quad was able to drop off and so bring back the news.

The first gun of our convoy is halted 30 yards from a bend in the road, the gun swung into position, some rounds unloaded and the gunners warned "Tank Alert". The following guns take up similar positions further back, each gun covering a bend in the road. Howitzer versus Tanks. A quick firing 18 pounder with its fixed ammunition has been known to disable tanks, but a slow Howitzer, with its separate charges which have to be loaded separately after the shell has been rammed home. Only 30 yards distance to cover if the tank doesn't stop the first shell. The leading tank swings round the bend, and a loud report answers as John Ogden, gun layer, pulls back his firing lever. The shell goes well home – the tank is halted. The following tanks, held up by their leader blocking the road, see the leader's hulk as a shield, their gun turrets firing over their disabled comrade. For a tank isn't harmless as soon as it's halted and held up. It becomes a fortress, it's armaments being it's cannon and machine guns. A Howitzer isn't portable like a rifle. John Ogden could only fire 6 more shells through the first tank to reach the second. Before the surviving Japs evacuate their tank to disappear into the woods with their machine guns, their cannon shells have taken an arm off our adjutant and killed the troops' most popular gun sergeant.

An information report with a captured Jap flag leaves RHQ for Division. It stated that the Enemy Tank break through is held, the crews rounded up and otherwise accounted for, and that the type of tank is estimated as being - in weight - 18 tons. It does not mention (because it isn't worth the mentioning) that the above mentioned Tank has a plate on it's side reading "Geo. Smith & Co, Birmingham, Eng".

A point in passing. Thanks to the Japs' British made tanks and American built planes, over half Malaya is in their hands. And the reason why the British are falling back before Birmingham's tanks and Uncle Sam's planes is because the British have not got a single tank of their own with which to retaliate and have not yet seen a British plane engage the enemy.

7 January 1942 : We had been doing local defence patrol whilst the convoy had formed up under cover of darkness on to the road. What a job with the heavy ammo trucks sinking time and again to their axle in the slush. We clambered into the last crowded truck, crowded for it held 5 Gurkhas, tired after their experiences of the day when their line had been broken by tanks and planes, they had of course a rifle as a defence against such things, and also a couple of 137 Regiment chaps for their battery but 250 men had been lost when they had been caught napping in their Wagon lines. "The tanks let us off pretty light then" I said, when I heard this. "Yes" came a retort from the other side of the truck's dark interior, "...except that we've lost Colonel Brocklehurst, forward RHQ with 18 signallers". Those tanks certainly did their stuff before they had reached us.

9 January 1942 : "We are going to surrender !" God! I knew things have been bad, one long series of strategic withdrawals. I expect to see the last stop, Singapore, on every new issue map, as the maps we have no longer cover the country which we are covering. Literally being pushed off the map. However 'surrender' proves to be "Serendah" the name of a village near our next position.

The heavy rains which fall every day have already soaked through our monsoon capes as we move in. The ground is a quagmire, the guns sink and the deep tyre tracks - left by the quads - rapidly fill with rain and become streams. Once in position, everybody digs – slit trenches, ammo pits, gunpits – and the quads, lighter now that they have lost their heavy guns and trailers, pull away to the shelter of the trees and the protection of their camouflage. Since we have had so many urgent moves, the quads never go far from the guns now. The School of Artillery says "....quads will harbour in Wagon Lines 2-4 miles in rear of the guns...." but this is jungle war, not Larkhill, Salisbury Plain. Trenches and pits completed, we soon discover they make excellent drainage slits for the surrounding land. Before the quick nightfall, guns are in position, laid on their lines, signal communications through and ready for the next order. For 7 hours we sit around in the dark waiting for a target but more important, waiting for the grub wagon, which has forgotten us for 17 hours. At past midnight, Q2 arrives with stew containers and hot tea. One at a time, the gunners and, we signallers, go over to draw our food for naturally phones and guns cannot be left unmanned whilst everyone has his meal. After a drenching, how cheered the hot stew and tea makes us. One man however isn't feeling so rosy as the others. For Geordie Scott had made a 50 yards excursion through the slush, dark and treacherous twigs, and had drawn his food and safely made a return journey to his gun. As he entered his gunpit, he stepped - in the darkness – down a pothole. His tea, which I'll wager was worth a million dollars to him, shot forward and was lost in the puddles and the darkness. I wonder how he relived his feelings for Geordie seldom swears.

14 January 1942 : A quiet week. Quiet in that we have not been engaging any targets. We have been mostly on the move the past two days, taking up positions and then off again before a round is fired. The whole Army seems on the Southward Trek. It seems to be a withdrawal of both the East and West fronts down the roads converging onto Kuala

Lumpur. We seem to be trying to cover too wide a front, the infantry can only deploy a mile either side of the roads whilst the Japanese infiltrate round them through the jungle paths led by Malayan guides. An example was Serendah where Jap guerrillas were in the village with British infantry still the far side of it. Thanks to Colonel Gold, (Colonel since we lost Colonel Murdoch and RHQ at Slim), our signal trucks reeling in lines were given timely warning and cut the cables thus avoiding falling in their hands. The journey hasn't been without incident – no journey is with the Jap planes flying lower and cheekier every day. We came through KL shortly after midnight with the bridges about to be blown. Bdr Downie in his bren gun carrier is missing and unless he got across before the bridges went, he will be cut off. KL was being looted wholesale by troops and natives. A few glowing buildings burning steadily showed that a half hearted 'scorched earth' policy was being carried out. At Kuala Luang, we pitch our tents, unpack and maintain equipment, do some washing and prepare for a rest. We are told we may rest for maybe a month, perhaps only a fortnight but certainly not less than a week. Thus assured, we prepare to settle down and get an early reveille next morning, with the latest orders 'Prepare to move'. We are off again.

16 January 1942 : We are off to stop a new Jap force just landed behind us at Batu Pahat on the coast. We take up a position but yield it to B Battery who have a longer range with their 25 pounders than our 4.5 howitzers. Now B Battery is in the thick of it and cut off with 5 Japanese defended road blocks to prevent aid. The infantry had already cleared previous road blocks and our ammunition trucks and ambulance went up. I have seen the 19 bullet holes the ambulance collected on the way up.

23 January 1942 : At Ayer Hitam we are holding an unhealthy spot for apart from being on the crossroads, the same trees that conceal us, shelter an ammunition point, divisional signals and brigade HQ. No wonder the planes pay us so much attention. When the first 7 bombers rained down and made the ground tremble with the thud of their bombs, but doing no damage, something dawned on a RASC driver sheltering beneath his ammo truck. "Do you know" he confided "when that Chinese coolie went past on the road with a split pack of rice leaving a trail of rice, it struck me then as being fishy". Stupid fool, did the RASC driver not know the rice trail signal to aircraft is an old 5th column trick used during this war. Our gunners know this is a touchy spot and no pains are spared in disguising guns into harmless hedges. I myself, have cut 15 papaya trees down for GE's benefit and nearly got us all bitten to death with red ants. Wally turned his fire extinguisher onto them and after the chemicals had done their deadly work, hundreds of new red ants turned up and carried off the bodies ! A distant hum swells into a drone and 7 planes flying low sweep round over us. We are making rapid mental calculations of the number of necessary strides to the nearest trench, when a murmuring grows into a cheer which sweeps on as neighbouring troops take it up. "British Planes. They're British. The glamour boys are here". The first planes we've seen are as good as a tonic.

24 January 1942 : Alternative Position. GE and two guns are harbouring below in the dell – we might take up a section position here. I am doing perimeter guard, that is patrolling the woods round the top of the bowl in which the guns are harboured some 200 yards distance below. I should come off shortly, it seems hours since I came on. Already it is dark and I've had to drop my turn ups and lower my shirt sleeves to prevent mosquito bites. Guards should be doubled at dusk but no extra man has yet shown himself. Through watching the fireflies twinkling through the trees I find I can make out two shadowy figures approaching. I snap my safety catch forward but they are gone. Hell – why doesn't my relief come up. I hear a thin voice shouting from the bowl below. I can just make out "Holt – come down". I shouted "OK" and stumble down through the bomb shattered trees, and eventually, guided by his twinkling torch, come up to an apologetic Dinky Durnford, our new GPO. "I am awfully sorry Holt" he explains as he leads me to GE on the road. "We left this position 2 hours ago. If Limb had not remembered you had been left behind, you might be there till Dooms day". After Jitra, this makes the second time GE has left me behind.

26 January 1942 : The past two days has seen us again on the move with what seems like the Army on the road. Miles of rattling infantry brengun carriers, Indian troop transports and British Artillery. A second Aussie supply convoy is going forward against the stream on the road to supply the newly formed Aussie front. For since Muar River, the Aussies have come into the fighting and are now doing their stuff. At Ayer Hitam, we read in the Singapore Times that the Japs had claimed another landing 25 miles from Johore Bahru, and now a couple of days after their claim and our denial, it has actually materialised, so it looks like most of us are heading for Johore Bahru. Our journey has taken us through Malacca State and through some of the more deserted parts of Malaya with nothing but jungle country coming right to the road's edge. We have come through flooded country too with our motorcycles seizing up with water in their carburettors and our trucks sending up bow waves like motor launches. This nautical episode pleased the four occupants in the ramshackled Chinese truck closely following us. In our cross truck discourse which passed between us on the move, we learned that they were four sailors, survivors of the 'Repulse', who had been doing guerrilla warfare with the infantry up country and now making their way to Singapore to try to get another ship.

JOHORE BAHRU

Now we are in Johore Bahru, the most southerly point of the Malayan peninsula after having come down Malaya's length, from the rice growing states bordering the jungle borderland of Thailand's frontier, the tin mining states, rubber growing states, the 'cat' country and wild country of Johore. 600 miles in 7 weeks ! We've heard the good news, that B Battery, which we gave up as lost at Batu Pahat, have had 3 days wandering in the jungle in their escape and have been rescued off the coast by a naval gunboat. They had escaped with the loss of their Major, guns and transport. I've had a chance of buying some boxes of chocolate bars and bread – two very welcome commodities. I've also sent a cable home from the town's cable office which is still open, reassuring all at home that I am OK and managed to visit the newly built hospital on the waterfront in the hopes of seeing my pal Will. But Will had just 12 hours previously been evacuated from the hospital for Singapore Island. The hospital, a fine modern, many storied structure, was being cleared of it's hundreds of wounded, the lobbies and floors impassable by the waiting stretcher cases on the floors and a countless stream of walking wounded filing down the stairs, black, white and yellow troops, being shepherded down to the transport on the road by the VAD nurses. I don't consider this a place for these plucky women – they should have all been evacuated off the island by now – at this 11th hour. Singapore Island, it's nearest point a mile across the water, is being well bombed, formations of 27 flying across at regular intervals. The civilian sirens remind me of 'Wailing Winnie' during my last leave home in London.

The Troop Officer called us together. "Tonight we are going over to the Island. The Army will be crossing the Causeway, which will be blown after the last troops, and we will prepare to hold the Island for a 2 year siege. You will have till 7 o'clock tonight to requisition corrugated sheeting and everything suitable for holding water. You've not much time – so get moving". And thus, I became a legalised gangster, riding on the floorboard of the truck slowly patrolling the streets of Johore Bahru. Song Heng Kee – Ironmongers - just our ticket. 5 of us jump off, whilst the truck drives on dropping men off at likely places. Never was a shopkeeper more surprised when the 5 of us entered his shop and started taking away the washing baths piled in his shop. Since nobody was bothering with an explanation to Mr Song Heng Kee, I ventured to explain to him that we were only requisitioning his baths for the Army. 3 times I explained until suddenly enlightened, he beamed and said, "In that case, we will give him chitty please". Well all the other shopkeepers were calling native policy and British Military Police over to stop this looting and all Song Heng Kee wanted was a "chitty please". I obliged signing a receipt for the baths with my worthless name and rank which carried no weight as a gunner. I felt tempted to make it out to the IJA for little did the shopkeeper know the only Army shortly to be in the town would be the Imperial Japanese Army.

Chapter Fourteen

SINGAPORE ISLAND

30 January 1942

Besieged on Singapore Island. Civil air raid sirens have ceased, wailing warnings for raids are too frequent and continuous for timely warnings. I always thought Jap planes never flew at night but last night I was convinced otherwise. Hardly have the last troops crossed the Causeway, blowing it behind us, when one of their night reccy planes came gliding over with engines cut off. Our first warning was the sudden thrumming of surrounding Bofors and brens, beautiful red and green tracer shells and bullets climbing slowly up through the night to heaven. Trapped in the sudden arm of a search light, we saw the plane – low, silent and gleaming silver. At sight of the quarry, the ack acks drum tattoo intensified. The plane slipped and rattled it's guns down the beam. As quickly as it had stabbed the darkness, so was it as quickly extinguished. A cough and a roar and Johnny Jap's engine came to life and it was away to the mainland.

Today we have had our first experience of 'sluice bombing'. Our half-prepared position was in a clearing, the incomplete gunpits and trenches gaping open and exposed. Hitherto, the familiar 27 bombers have flown straight over us bound for Singapore Town, but this morning as we watched the formation "25, 26, 27 all there!" we heard a new sound above the drone. It sounded at first like a tap running, growing louder and louder till it had swollen to the intensity of a gushing waterfall. We recognised it not as the familiar swish of a stick of bombs but the gush of an avalanche of them. I was sitting at my set in the truck at the time and was so held by the time it was taking for them to land and was so certain we were the obvious target that I just sat awaiting the end. Maybe we were the target. Anyhow, rightly or wrongly, the village in front of us got it. Thud after thud after thud shook the ground, every thud nearer and the swish of more coming. The last thud finally crunched barely 100 yards away, our only share being stray splinters of spent shrapnel and a cloud of blue smoke and fumes. This bomb swamping of a target is something new for us.

2 February 1942 : The Japs, masters of Malaya are probably wondering on their next move. I've had a jolly time helping to dig OP's on the shore near the Naval Base. Naturally our digging must be as unobtrusive as possible both from the air and from the opposite shore. An OP is the eyes of the battery and if the OP is known to the enemy, the guns are soon left without an OP to direct it's gunfire. I am doing 24 hours relief with the OP signaller, for it is gruelling work manning an OP, constantly alert yet remain unseen. During 2 hours off today, I slipped into a vacated Naval Admiral's house and enjoyed the luxury of his bath, wallowing in it despite the sudden outside racket of bombers, bombs, shells and fighters. If a bomb was going to hit the house, I would die clean. The bath over, I had the pleasure of using the Admiral's talcum powder and ransacked his drawers before I climbed into his best blue Celanese underwear. That night back in the cramped damp OP trench, we watched the lights of the Japanese Army trucks across the strip of water on the opposite shore and clearly heard from across the water, the sounds of the Japs wood sawing and hammering. I wondered if they could hear our movements as easily.

5 February 1942 : We are leaving this position in front of the Ack Acks for Nei Soon village. A pity, since we have put a lot of work into the position completing deep dugouts, gunpits and ammo slits. We had even started on a cement command post. Sgt Heaver, the Army's best scrounger had not only pinched a contractors truck, but had used it to transport 2 truckloads of sand for the cement which he had twigged from a Sand Merchant under the name of a non-existent 30th A/A Regimental RA. Since the death of Sgt Keen, Sgt Heaver has been doing Troop QMS. His 'requisitioned' goods include a stock of clothing he swiped from the Naval Base and about 30 cwts of tinned food and a lorry he took to carry it in.

The sky is overcast with an oily black pall fed by a pillar of smoke rising from the burning Naval Base oil tanks. I saw that lot go up the morning before last. At 4 in the morning (I was manning the phones), I heard a solitary low plane circle above. Obviously ours I thought. Then came the thud of a bomb, a brilliant white flash which shimmered a few seconds and the boom of a violent explosion. As the fire got under way, the glow turned crimson reflecting into clouds of billowy black smoke. Now the bombers are using this as a smokescreen and our fighters are very busy not escaping loss. Only this morning, one fighter returned with its undercarriage dangling like a pendulum as it circled for the 'drome.

6 February 1942 : We should hold the Island for recent reinforcements (18th Div), more than replace the casualties we had on the mainland. Dug in 2 miles from the coast, our guns cover the opposite shore alongside Johore Bahru. Our OP has been observing movements across the water. Our guns, below a crest should be invisible from the opposite shore yet hardly have we fired when one, two, three, four regular explosions from a Jap battery returning our fire, sound from our right. Our OP, seeing the smoke of their guns pass down a counter battery target. In reply to our gunfire comes once more the wavering whistle and quickening whine as their next four shells land nearer to us, but still to the right. Obviously they are searching for us. A sudden whine and crash and a shell lands less than 20 yards from N° 4 gun. If that was a ranging shell we were sunk but no fire for effect follows it up. Our artillery dual finishes up with their guns silenced. From the OP comes news that Observation Balloons are being sent up across the water.

7 February 1942 : Jap heavies are shelling all points on the island concentrating on the airfields. We learn that with their airfields rendered useless, the RAF are evacuating to Java or Sumatra. With no air support again and our every movement watched by the balloons, the Japs have us in a ticklish spot again. The night has been hideous with the thunder of heavy bombardment on our left. Today we hear the Aussies had been shelled all night and the Japs have invaded the island under the barrage. Hand to hand fighting is in progress. Meanwhile all sorts of Jap artillery are getting to work, light stuff searching for troop positions, heavy stuff shining slowly overhead for Singapore Town. With new Jap forces behind us at Buketima 8 miles away, we may have to fall back from the Causeway. This will allow them to bridge the gap in the Causeway and bring across tanks. The Island's water reservoirs will soon be in their hands. Meanwhile the planes, knowing once more the RAF are gone, are more active than ever. Things aren't exactly hunkey dorey.

13 February 1942 – BUCKLEY AVENUE

Singapore has never seen the likes of this before. The European houses and gardens which, only 2 weeks ago, would have reminded me of London's suburbia, now seem to have become mixed up with guns, troops and ammo supply points. The houses of Buckley Avenue form a sedate row, their gardens backing onto a playing field. From practically every back garden peeps a gun. Artillery is plentiful now that the troops are ringing a small circle round the town. The veranda of this house will be our command post and into this we have run the various lines and connected up the various phones. Our unoccupied minutes we spend in sandbagging for slit trenches, are impossible with a water level of 18 inches below the ground. Throughout the day bomber formations have been making continuous raids. The bofors ack ack sprinkled around are acting splendidly, the gunners pumping hundreds of shells up onto a protective screen against low level attacks. Field artillery are active too. The houses around throw back 3 resounding echoes for every one crack of a gun or bark of a howitzer. And there, suspended in the sky a couple of miles away, hang the observation balloons watching our movements and directing their artillery with disturbing accuracy. Dusk caught us firing with our rifles into a patrol we could see 200 yards away. Not before one of the patrol was killed did it become known it was only a returning British patrol. Throughout the night we hear close bren and tommy gun fire and the swish of their bullet streams suggesting Jap patrols are busy under cover of darkness. To add to the confusion, native traitors are sniping our troops from the houses, and throughout all this, the civilians are trying to carry on, with shells, bombs and bullets in the very streets they live in. The Australian woman in this house is a heroine – never once has she shown fear although she must know things are critical and war is literally on her doorstep. The Japs are very near for our ammo trucks have been ambushed on their way to our previous position where we left some HE.

Monday 16 February 1942 : This morning as we sit around on the tennis court, our surrendered rifles heaped in a pile, we have time to think over the past 48 hours or contemplate the future. The BBC announcing from a wireless in a house across the way, has given out that Singapore is fighting on and still holds out. Yet we had orders to destroy our guns half past 4 yesterday afternoon, and last night when we were lining the ditches with rifles in what we thought would be a fight to the last man, we got the official Unconditional Surrender order. The reasons being – No food, No water and humane reasons. For in 2 days shelling of the town, 8,000 civilians had become casualties. A day of spasmodic shelling had been followed by a night of heavier shelling. The first shell took us by surprise. With a crack sounding almost above us, a round landed in the lawn of the American woman's house behind us on which we had some of our trucks parked. They either had our range or were firing blind for an unexpected number of rounds of gunfire burst around.

One of the quads went up with a roar, it's load of ammunition making it an added danger. A petrol wagon was hit, the wagon was outside the Battery Command Post and the vivid white glow attracted further shelling. And thus the house acting as our BCP got hit destroying communications to the troops. Capt. Eustace left us to superintend work on the blazing quad, the last we saw him alive. We three signallers, Jack Warner, Ray Limb and myself had arranged our phone reliefs for the night and Jack had suggested resting off duty in the outhouse near the quads. When I had suggested this was too far from the phones in an emergency we shifted our kit from it. A little later it was a heap of rubble and bricks. However we never escaped altogether for Ray Limb and myself finally pitched our blankets on the flagstones alongside the house when a shell hit the next house but one. We were lying trying to sleep before our next turn on duty and with a gasp that he was hit, Limb went to get up. I too, at the same time had felt something punch the sole of my boot and fearing the worst, I hobbled to the veranda while others helped Ray Limb. They took Ray away with a nasty hip wound. Regarding myself, a splinter of shrapnel some 4 inches long by an inch wide had passed clean through the sole of my boot as I lay on my blanket and had lodged itself between my big and 2nd toe. The only damage was where the hot metal had burnt the flesh away on either toes. I was lucky it had not hit my toes but passed between them. Throughout the night, shells landed around us, the more distant giving short warning whines and the heavies lumbering slowly high overhead to spread the inferno in the docks which for 2 nights had daubed the night sky with crimson red. We could recognise a mortar, actually hearing the mortars a few seconds before it's projectile burst among us – entirely different to gunfire where the landing shell is the first hint.

Yesterday, in the first light of dawn, we started reorganising ourselves and speeding up our sandbagging. The ammo dump on our left was still burning, the crackling of thousands of bursting bullets sounding about the crackle of the flames. The 25 pounder batteries alongside us were perilously short of ammo with no more available and our 4.5 howitzers were now taking over their targets. At 4pm, our Major looking grave came and spoke with the GPO and the No 1s were called. We suspected something amiss for the 25 pounder battery alongside had ceased firing and had pulled the guns onto the playing field in front and were preparing to destroy them. Then we were told we were going to surrender. "...and all your paybooks and all kit with the Yeomanry crest or name marked, must be destroyed for the Japanese have promised the 155 complete annihilation (over the wireless) for the part we played in the Malayan campaign". And so went many of my treasured personal letters etc. "What are you going to do" said Wally. The gunners had spiked their guns and I had just destroyed my signalling equipment putting my hammer through £150 of wireless equipment and £50 of telephones, lamps and helio. With the guns silent, the quietness was uncanny. Burning equipment and bonfires could be seen everywhere in the streets and lawns – everything of value to an enemy going up in smoke. Four bombers, with no opposition from the destroyed ack ack guns, swooped and let their bomb-loads screech down. It looked like we would receive no mercy and our only arms now were rifles. I threw away my kit and with a rifle and 300 rounds I prepared to make my way to the docks. But I never got far for MPS were turning men back and the Military Police were turning machine guns on troops trying to leave the island by boat. The order was all men keep with their regiments. And as a regiment we lay as infantry in the ditches uncertain that we would be taken as prisoners, prepared for the worst and expecting it. And at 8.30 pm we got General Percival's order. "Lay down your arms, unconditional surrender". And so, what now.

Although many of our men we knew as comrades are dead,

we think it the biggest pity that we have lost Paddy Carrole. He had survived the Tank attack and other narrow escapes and got killed by a shell a few hours before surrender. My sympathy too with the Chinese now that the Jap troops are in the town all flushed with their victory. We have already seen a string of Chinese tied by their wrists being marched off by a Jap for execution with his British brengun over his shoulder. Apparently they were caught taking food from our abandoned trucks and looting is punishable with death.

19 February 1942 : Roberts Barracks are not too badly damaged despite the recent shelling. My foot would not allow me to march the 27 miles here from Singapore with the regiment, so I smuggled myself onto the one truck allowed to transport the regiment's kit. My last view of Singapore Town resembled a Gala Day in Tokyo, for from every house and window fluttered a Japanese flag to welcome the invader. If this was a true emblem of the peoples' feelings, our fight had been in vain. Most of the Chinese civilians wore handkerchiefs tied over their noses to keep off the sweat sickly stench of putrefying corpses in the streets. Outside the town we passed some Jap artillery which had helped create such havoc, long barrelled field pieces of about 3 and a half inch calibre. Here, in Roberts Barracks, the water supply is dislocated and severe rationing in force for cooking purposes only - and this is the dry season. The hot sun increasing your thirst and making you lose more moisture in sweat, but apart from this, considering things aren't properly organised for us yet, there is nothing to complain at, at all for these conditions.

Chapter Fifteen

CHANGI

22 February to 3 March 1942

We are temporarily quartered in Changi Gaol, 3 men to a cell. My pall Will, who recently rejoined the unit when the hospitals were cleared, still looks shaky. His leg is far from healed for his kneecap was removed and the knee joint seems fused. This should right itself with time. Will and Vic (still suffering from shell shock), are sharing the cell with me. We give Will the privilege of the concrete slab bed (these cells were meant for 1 native prisoner). Vic and myself sleeping on the floor either side. Things aren't organised yet and the regiment is still living on the tinned foods we held onto after capitulation. This means 2 meals a day. Breakfast at 10 consists of a little tinned bacon, 3 biscuits and tea. Dinner at 6 means some meat and vegetable stew and biscuits. I now know what hunger is. Every spoonful we take from our plate is masticated thoroughly and the hole thus made in the foot on the plate is filled over with the remaining food to make the plateful look no less. To my hungry eyes, even the Japanese flag above the gaol (a white flag with a red circle) reminds me of a fried egg.

7 March 1942 : We spent a couple of nights billeted in a bungalow overlooking the sea before moving on to the permanent camp at Changi. By day we sunbathed or looked for coconuts and by night preferred sleeping outside the bungalow under the stars, with a full tropical moon shimmering a thousand reflections in the sea. Both mornings found us burying a string of corpses washed up with the tide. They were bodies of Chinese, tied together and their hands behind their backs.

April 1942 : We are comfortable in this camp, for this was formerly a temporary British camp for the reinforcements for this country. The bungalows in which we sleep are wooden structures some 100 feet long and 20 feet wide, with 5 windows either side and 3 doors along it's length. The roofing is thatch made from the broad palm leaf of the coconut palms. It is perfect for keeping off the heat of the scorching sun but is just strong enough to withstand the heavy torrential downpours. Normally these huts house 30 men but we are not so spaced now for 70 men share the hut. The huts are sheltered in a bowl or valley for this wartime camp had been built with a view to concealment. But we have a padang or playing field on some high level ground in the camp. I appreciate this for games make a welcome diversion in the cooler dusk hours and nothing is finer than a moonlight walk around this field catching the cool breeze which comes in from the sea before the bugle's 'Lights Out' dismisses us down to the bungalows.

The camp which is bounded with a barbed wire apron 9 feet deep, holds the 2000 artillery men of the 11th Division. We are field and antitank with a number of Corps troops. Facing us across the road are the Australians who are camped in stone buildings of various types. The road runs through to the Infantrymen (British) of the 18th Division who probably are the least fortunate for they are in tents and various billets. And behind the Aussies and the 18th are Roberts Barracks which is being used as a hospital for those troops slowly recovering from war wounds or who have already fallen to the diseases liable to be contracted in the camps. We do our own guards but the roads between the camps are patrolled by the Sikh sentries, traitors, who after Capitulation went over to the Jap Cause and who are now prepared to fight their former allies. The whole of the prison areas have an outer perimeter wire patrolled by Japanese Guards. So while we enjoy freedom in a sense, for we are under our own officers' administration, we are thrice guarded. Firstly by our own guards (unarmed of course), secondly by the Sikh sentries who patrol between the camps, and thirdly, the outer ring of Jap guard houses. But this is a pleasant corner of the island, hardly war scarred and forever looking green and fruitful, heavy foliage alongside the road and coconut groves between us and the sea.

9 May 1942 : Now that my foot is at long last healed, I am fit for full duties. Today I was on 'Rations'. Going down to Changi Pier for rice is no light fatigue for it means pushing and pulling our trailer up and down hills for a distance of three and a half miles and after loading one and a quarter tons of rice in 2 cwt sacks, there is the hell of a pull back. The trailers are Army trucks which have had their engines removed and all surplus fittings stripped off to lighten the weight. Then by running two rope traces from the front with bamboo crosspoles at intervals along each rope, a squad of men can do the work of a horse team. In this way, all our transport for the camp we pull ourselves like human mules. The trailers are used for such jobs as collecting the firewood that the tree felling squad cut outside the camp, or bringing up the bins of salt water we fetch from the sea.

For salt is necessary and we get so little so by boiling our rice in sea water, we extract the salt from the sea. However, to keep to the point, on our way to Changi Pier, we have to pass through the Aussie Lines, the Hospital area and the Southern area. All parties which leave their own camp wire must only do so under the permit of the Jap ferry flag carried by the officer of the party. Whenever I pass through these other camps, I am always on the look out for faces I may know. In the 18th Division camp, I found Tom Griffiths. Tom was in the 92nd and was transferred with me to the 155th. His bunk was next to mine in Lanark and he was my friend. We both tried to get out of the regiment together. I failed but he succeeded and when we left him behind when we came abroad, he was sent to Woolwich and joined the 148th. He came abroad and landed in Singapore 2 weeks before it fell and only saw action for one week before he became prisoner. And now we are both together again in the same PoW camp. It's a small world. Our load was too much of a pull on the way back up the hills so we came back the long way round on the level road through the 18th Division. It was heavy work for the sun and food don't give us much energy. I often wonder what our people at home would think if they saw us, a squad of men like a mule team, pulling a trailer and load, heads down pulling steadily and taking paces all together in step to even the pull, and a bath of sweat running down your body to saturate the waistband of your shorts. We pass, this way, the British Cemetery, filling up all too fast, for the prisoners who have died in captivity. The cemetery squad are doing a nice job of work. At first, when dysentery was carrying off such a toll among us, the graves were hastily dug in the waste ground alongside the road, overgrown with brush and grass. But the whole area is now being cleared over and around the graves and the cemetery laid out with green turf, rolled paths and flower beds. Each grave has a simple wooden cross bearing name, number, age and the date.

The cemetery will eventually link up with the Australian cemetery further along the road. The Aussie graves are very simply marked with a cross bearing the man's regimental number only. It looks so impersonal.

15 May 1942 : I had thought at first that a PoW life would be a life penned behind barbed wire and left to pass time as best you might. Far from it. We have half of us away on working parties road building at Buketima and the fatigues in the camp are countless. Here are some of the jobs I have done in and around the camp. Every 3rd morning before the sun has started to climb high and strong, I have helped fell the trees with axe or crosscut saw for firewood with which to boil our rice. Ration parties come twice a week. Salt water is a 2 hours job and daily we grind rice through a wringer to get rice flour for baking. Wood must be split when it has been brought in. Latrines must be bored in 20 foot holes in the ground. There are countless digging jobs in the camp, monsoon trenches to catch the torrential rain and to prevent it flooding the lower part of the camp, digging and preparing agricultural plots for potatoes. Every 3rd day we fall for an outside working Jap party. Then we have our turn at 24 hour Gate Guards and there are numerous jobs in the camp, church building and other building jobs. At least 4 hours a day are spent in necessary work for the life of the camp. The work which has brought me the most benefit was the job I have just completed. There were some 20 foot 5 inch by 4 inch beams brought in for building a ration store. Last night, Will and myself paid a visit to the site and carried 2 beams away and put them beneath our bungalow for safe keeping. Today I scrounged a couple of rice sacks which I washed and dried in the sun. I have now completed for myself a bed with a sacking as a bed canvas. It is so much better than sleeping on the floor for no matter how much you can punch the floor boards, they don't get any the softer. Our only trouble now is the bugs. The billet has bags of black bugs and if they get into my bed, I will let the ants get into the bed and kill the bugs. But then I must think of a way to rid the bed of the ants! Flies by day, mosquitos and bugs by night – it seems we were born to be tormented.

27 May 1942 : Possess a thing and it dwindles in value. Lose it and it assumes the value of the world. I never realised how much my home and parents meant to me when I was living at home but this enforced life away from the things and the ones I love has shown me the value of all which I formerly took for granted in it's true perspective. It is the thought of home which keeps us going. If a place is worth living for, it is worth fighting for and it has taken me on a journey half way round the globe to convince me undoubtedly that there is no place like home.

Changi:
Poem to my Mother :

Good Intentions

Praise God, Mother, that He'll us spare
Till with these days of madness done
We'll have the greatest joy to share
That joy – at long last coming home.

And I'll come home a better son
The family life we knew is gone
It's war torn gap cannot be filled
Rose and Lily since wed, Young Tom dead.

He served so young ere he was killed
At home, I'm now the only one
These days of hardship teach me this
To love my home and not forget.

Your love and sacrifices made
When I was young, I'll pay that debt
For here and now, I make this vow
That I'll come home a grateful son.

For many years, you've had to scrape and toil
So that I might enjoy good clothes, good school,
good food and such
That built me up a healthy boy
Your work at home was never done.

Because of all your loving care
I had strong health, thus fortified
I've had a better change to fight
These gruelling times whilst others die.

Your work is done
Mine's just begun
When I return a prodigal son.

(PAGE CUT OUT OF DIARY)

19 June 1942 : What a glorious sunrise today. After Tiffin, I was resting before the afternoon's fatigues began when Captain Sewell came into the billet with some Japanese postcards. "You are allowed to send one message home" he said. "The Jap conditions say the message must be brief and readable at a glance. If you spoil your card, you have lost your opportunity of writing home". With only 10 minutes or so in which to write the card, I fumbled for a safe message. Finally I decided on "Dear Mum, Dad, Lily and Rose. I am safe, healthy, under good conditions. Keep as happy as I am keeping. Have faith until I come home again. Until then, my deepest love. Cheerio. Keep smiling. Will". I hope to God it arrives for they last heard from me in action 7 months ago. They always fear the worst although I've often advised them by word and in my letters that "No news is good news". (Pencil remark in margin of diary that the card never arrived home).

2 July 1942 : Many happy returns Dad. Today I was out again on Jap working party. Just before dawn, Bdr O'Connor twigged my foot and I tumbled from bed straight away for I only had 20 minutes in which to wash, sweep my bed space and make up my bed for daily billet inspection. I breakfasted on the usual mug of tea (minus sugar and milk), a large ladle of rice boiled in water and a rice chapatti and rissole. The chapatti is simply ground rice boiled and browned into cakes over a hot plate, the rissole being a cake of boiled rice flavoured with peanuts or whitebait and fried in Ghee. As the sun began to climb, the party - some 100 men strong - fell in and moved off in threes down the road, our chunkals, picks and spades over our shoulders. The 3 mile march along the road which is bordered right to the road edge by hedges or trees, might have been pleasant under different circumstances for it always reminds me of the lanes in summer back home in Surrey or Sussex. The Sikh sentry we passed got his salute from us (Jap orders) and he salaamed over his bayonet. He must get satisfaction to see "superior white sahibs" reduced to this. We must have seemed a non-descript party. For my own part, I was wearing a pith helmet I found, after capitulation, and was stripped to the waist (as was everybody), my shorts were reasonable enough and I was wearing Wellington boots I found in an Admiral's house.

But no 2 men were dressed alike. Some were hatless, others wore Aussie sundowners, toupees, side-hats, sailor caps and anything they might have found since 15 February. For our head-dress were steel helmets up to that date but tin hats are no good for tropical head-dress. Many were bearded but now razor blades are available clean chins might be compulsory again. Footwear was pretty ragged in some cases and although we started off with a smart 'left right', sloppy boots and loose soles soon reduced the step to a ragged amble. We repair our boots with soles shaped from cut up motor tyres. Rubber soles would wear well but unfortunately the nails seldom bind the rubber sole to the boot for longer than a fortnight. Half hours marching brought us to the outer perimeter wire where our Jap guards were awaiting us. We have got to know them by now for they are the same men every time, corporals and sergeants from the Jap Military.

We marched on again, our guards hurrying alongside with their short steps to keep up with us. They wear a round toupee well down on the head without any extension to protect the nape of the neck. Their khaki shirts are marked on the arm by the white arm band and black triangle of the Military police. The rank is marked by the number of stars on a red background on their breast. The white tab with the column of queer symbols on their right breast is their identity disc. They carry a bayonet and either wear long shorts or knee breeches - their legs allowing no air to their knees or body. When we passed Changi Gaol (now housing the white civilians), we could see a woman or girl watching through the bars of the third landing. Poor beggars – we waved them a cheery greeting. At long last we reached our work by a path across country through the wood. We were split into the usual squad, each squad under the Jap. My job today was carrying the logs, another squad was cutting, some 400 yards to the wiring squad who were using the logs as stakes and piles. I tried to get the wiring job for it is the easiest – only you get cut with the barbed wire a lot. To hell with log carrying, it's heavy work on rice, and grazes the skin off your shoulder. The blasted sun doesn't help things either. We have a 10 minute break every hour to sit in the shade. We got conversing to our guard improving his smattering of English and got him talking of his wife - whom he hadn't seen for 5 years, China and anything to make him forget when the ten minutes rest was over. We learnt he was a journalist. The others are (or were) police detectives or other equally educated callings. We chatted for 25 minutes - until when he bent his arm to demonstrate a jiu-jitsu hold, he saw his wrist watch. With a hurried order he shooed us to our work – but we hadn't done bad, 15 minutes extra rest. At midday break I ate my 3 chapattis and 2 rissoles washing it down with black tea. Normally, after dinner until we start again, we look for coconuts or ramatam fruit. But today the guards had brought along a camera. They picked the tallest of us, myself included and posed with us - even the officer complete with jackboots and sword. I suppose I will now adorn a Tokyo mantelpiece. This afternoon, I was on clearing squad, cutting brush. This is a hell of a job if the red ants are there in hundreds, ready to torment you as they fall on your back every time you shake the tree with your axe blows. We burnt an ant infested hedge and thinking the smoke would hide me from the guard the other side of the hedge, I snooped off to open a green coconut for a drink. But he saw me through the smoke and shouted hell for me to come back. Had I been within arms length of him, I would have caught his backhander. And it's a foolish man who tries to resist their punishment. It is amusing when a squad is caught slacking. The guilty squad must line up in a ditch and the Jap, in order to reach up, walks along the top of the ditch slapping each face in turn. Face slapping is strange and resentful to us but it is in order for the Nipponese Army. It is nothing for even a Jap officer to be slapped by a superior if guilty of some small disciplinary fault. I do object to the Sikhs face slapping and man-handling the prisoners though, for they were never slapped when they were with the Army. At long last, 5 o'clock came and we checked our tools (thank heavens we weren't delayed looking for lost wire cutters or such like) and marched back. On passing Curren Camp, the Sikh traitor HQ, we saw white troop prisoners cleaning their latrines out. It's a poor unfortunate who gets sent there for punishment. Forced to sleep on the ground without blankets or groundsheet and the scapegoat for them to relieve their anti British hatred. It was 6 o'clock when we arrived back and after a wash and dinner of rice and thin stew, I turned in. The day hadn't been exceptionally hard but the continual sun saps all energy from you.

1 August 1942 : I enjoy these fishing fatigues. We go down to the sea as a party of 5 men under the Fishing Officer who has knocked about this part of the world for years. He knows Java and Borneo well and can speak all the local dialects around Changi, both Malayan and Chinese. The fish we catch goes to the hospital for the sick. Naturally, the Japs will not allow us to have a boat for fishing, so we just dropped our shorts onto the beach and waded or swam out to the tide traps that we erected on previous days. The water is quite pleasant for the hot sun overhead always keeps the water a nice warm temperature. The traps are two long lines of wall made of wire mesh and built at a right angled shape like a letter 'L', running out to sea some two hundred yards from the shore. The arm of the 'L' sweeps across the tides flow. The fish swim in with the incoming tide and are hemmed in by the wall of mesh when the tide recedes. They are forced to swim to the right angle of the 'L' and through a gap into the cage or trap. We could wade out up to our chests but swimming is easier. The trap we lifted today was a trouble for it had become entangled and kept us standing in the water for two hours with jelly fishes stinging our naked bodies. I felt like I had lain naked in a bed of nettles. We had about 40 lb of fish today – mostly mudfish and stinging rays. A ray is like a plaice with a rat like tail in which it harbours it's sting. Stinging fish have already caused the death of Sgt Halifax and lamed Bdrs Mais and Pratt for some 10 weeks – so they are no light foe to come against. There were plenty of crab fish too which we threw back but with the rays and mudfish we had a good catch. Very often though, we suspect the Chinese fisherman poached our traps before we came down. A few days ago, a fishing party had a young shark which was kept for the regiment. It was delicious, it tasted just like cod. When we at last had waded back to the beach, we found someone had pinched one of our water bottles – probably a native. We find queer things on this beach. Last time I tripped over a bone sticking out of the sand, an arm bone of a buried skeleton. There is also an unexploded mine washed up on the beach. It looks so tempting to look across the sea knowing freedom is across the ocean but the naval lookout post watches the beach and Jap patrols come through the coconut groves every so often. On the way back to camp, we stopped at Kampong where a villager sold us pineapples at nine cents and some banana fritters. We kept a sharp look out for Japs though for it is forbidden to trade or talk to native villagers. Once back in camp, I had my dinner and hurried over to the Divisional veranda for the Debating Society had an interesting motion....."That in the opinion of the house, Permanent Peace is Impossible". Much as it was against my preconceived ideas, the motion was carried. I trust this isn't really so.

20 August 1942 : At last I have got my staff job after weeks of waiting. I tried for this job because I got so fed up with the various jobs ordinary duty men were always falling for. When Sgt Gallagher of the RAMC said I would report to the Anti-Malarial squad (I applied weeks ago), I was as pleased as punch. The advantage of a staff job is that you have your own job to do and don't get messed around on fatigues all hours of the day. The squad of half a dozen men from the camp, led by 3 RAMC NCO's has the job of keeping down the mosquitos which cause Malaria in the camp. We go out daily in the surrounding jungle draining stagnant water in which they breed, filling in the numerous water holes and draining the land. This wet climate causes numerous water holes and lakes, which if they cannot be filled in, must be oiled to kill the mosquito larvae living in the water. When the young larvae swim to the surface for air, they get suffocated by the film of oil over the water. Today we went down to the mangrove swamps near the sea, for the tides keep the swamps fed with brackish water in which a dangerous mosquito breeds. It is always uncomfortable working in the sun but as we left the scrub and walked into the swamps, it was like entering a steaming bathroom. The humidity sent rivers of sweat down my body. The tide runs up into the low lying swamps by a channel. We thought we could drain the swamps by digging tributaries in the tide channel. Each swing of my chunkal sent up clods of stinking ooze. The suction of the mud made the digging hard but I find my Wellington boots fine for sloshy work. When at last only the last spade full of mud would open up the tributary into the channel, we all gathered around for the big moment when the brown swampy water would join the cleaner sea water in the channel. The last spade full came out with a sucking plop and instead of the swamp water draining into the sea, the sea water poured from the channel into the swamp ! However, there's always another day tomorrow in which to right the wrong. I found a coconut in the grove and picked a good pineapple on the way back to camp and so my labour for the day had not been entirely without reward.

September 1942 : POW Changi

September round again sees the 3rd anniversary of the war. Septembers in the past have seemed to be my fateful month. A few memory flashbacks recall that in September 1930 I started my 5 years schooling at Wilsons Grammer School, Camberwell, and passed up into each of the higher standards every following September, until September 1934. In September 1935 I started the only job I've ever had at the Ocean. In September 1938, my pal John Rawlings and myself made a trip to France. In September of 1939, I was mobilised into the Army two days before war was declared and on the 26th September, I landed in France. In September 1940, I received word that my home had had to be evacuated through a nearby aerial torpedo and I had a new place within a week. The last week of September I went home on leave, arriving home just as my young brother – doing voluntary ARP work – was killed in the bombings. September 1941 found me landing in Malaya. I have now to see what the following September holds for me. (Pencil note written in margin of diary reads September 1945 I left Taiwan a free man).

We recently had a parade lasting 5 hours in the sun awaiting the new Japanese General taking over PoWs. He gave us a speech in Japanese which - when interpreted, came down to 3 sentences – "You are going to be governed according to the regulations laid down by the great

Japanese Empire. I am now in command of the prisoners in these camps. I will, if you are dutiful and obedient, treat you generously and kindly accordingly within the framework of these regulations". Salutes all round, the Jap sentries bow and fall out, the convoy of flagged cars move off and we march back to our delayed dinner.

20,000 forms have been sent into the camps. We are expected to each sign a form for the Japs, promising never to escape under any circumstances. Of the 20,000 forms, only 3 have been signed and sent back.

Chapter Sixteen

THE SELARANG INCIDENT

September 1942

Selerang Incident (Taken from an additional notebook written by dad after the War)

Selerang Incident – introduced to me the spirit of our vanquished army. It rose great in Adversity.

We, 16,000 men, of the British and Australian forces, had been PoWs of 6 months standing – interned behind the barbed wire aprons of Changi area camps.

Our kit was still good, our boots kept in repair from WD tyres. Every night the story of the disastrous Malayan Campaign was still put under inquest round our home made oil lamps. The drums of oil came from the pits of the Coastal guns – the ones which had been fixed pointing the wrong way.

A trickle of news came from well secreted radio sets (constructed in water bottles) and became distorted with each telling and knocked well out of shape, to circulate the camps as 'bore hole news'.

Although the Japanese had started issuing rice as our ration, we still had our diet supplemented with European tinned food from foraging party trips. Every dusk, adventurous ones used to slip beneath the wire and visit the Chinese and Malayan Kampongs trading clothing and 'occupation' money to villagers in exchange for British Army tinned foods which most villagers had acquired from Army stocks when Singapore Capitulated.

These were traded in camp and were welcome to those who did not fancy the snails which were also being collected and cooked as a dietary supplement.

So when we were paraded and told by Major General Shimpei Fukuye that "You are going to be governed according to the regulations laid down by the Great Japanese Empire and if you are dutiful and obedient, you will be treated generously and kindly within these regulations", we felt pretty confident. Although not an organised Army, we maintained a discipline within ourselves, and, at Birdwood camp had NCO classes, marching drill and a hope that we would retake the island from within !!

Of every 100 men who heard the speech (we were aged mostly in our 20s), 73 were alive 3 years later. (Far East PoW statistics, I believe I am correct in saying were 27% dead as compared to 4% PoWs in Germany).

Then, the Awakening. Into the Camps came 16,000 forms. Each form was a declaration that no attempt would be made to escape under any circumstances. Each man was required to sign this undertaking.

Of the 16,000 forms, I think less than five were duly signed. We would be subjected therefore to 'measures of severity'.

Little indeed compared to subsequent years on the 'Railway' or in the Mines but severe enough.

All men would move to Selerang Barracks on 1st September – a Barrack block which had been built to house 800 British troops according to British Army standards.

The 2,000 men from our camp had less than half a mile to transport ourselves and our belongings, but our 2,000 arrivals had hardly looked askance at our cramped space when along came men of the 18th Division. They had a 2 mile walk and had towed the engineless chassis of Army trucks piled high with cookhouse boilers, kit and paraphernalia that is "all" to a PoW unit. Into Selerang Barrack square straggled this refugee column and had hardly squeezed in, then came the 11th Division. Came Southern Command, came Malayan Command, came the Australian Division, came 16,000 men of the British forces – 16,000 men to share the barracks which had once housed 800 men of the Gordon Highlanders. Put a quart in a pint pot and you spill half. Put 16,000 men in Selerang and you spill onto the roof (fortunately flat) and onto the Square – all over the Square. Standing room only.

By the Usages of War, a holding power cannot require a PoW to give his parole.

Having concentrated the area into one group of barrack blocks, the Japanese began to seal off the area. Each road was patrolled by Japanese or Sikh sentry units. The Sikhs were part of the Chandra Bose Indian Liberation Army – who were prepared to ally themselves with Nippon to fight the British. The Military Police (Japanese troops recognised as being the Kempetai by the black triangle on their arms), mounted machine gun posts, at strategic points. So now we can sweat it out.

My diary records my impression as I looked down from the roof. "The throngs remind me of the crowds on a Bank holiday Monday at the London Zoo – except that here we will not escape at the end of the day to the privacy of our own homes".

Yet even in this throng of thousands in apparent chaos, came a voluntary discipline and organisation, which probably explains our "planned economy" of today, as only being a national characteristic.

I am sure that with nationals of many other countries, jungle law would have emerged.

16,000 men in a barracks with no water laid on (supplies were broken during the fighting period). Daily temperature averages 90°.

Most men not yet hardened to a rice diet had loose bowels. Dysentery was a common complaint in the camps and the diet over the past 6 months had considerably lessened physical strength and resistance to disease. 16,000 men so far had no facilities to perform their natural functions.

Before night fall, work had started in the barrack square. Everybody somehow made room to enable pick and shovel squads to dig latrine trenches 30 feet long, 18 feet deep.

In a PoW camp, it is amazing how no matter what may be wanted, from a pick to a ladies dress, one will be forthcoming.

The first trench was wanted urgently, and had to be thrown open to use when only 10 feet deep. 40 trenches were needed and these, in 4 rows of 10, soon dominated the scene with the piles of upturned clay and sand. A Royal Engineer had located the run of a water main and had tapped in a point. I do not know if it is possible to form a queue into a mass of people, but I do know that through a dense mass of human beings, an orderly queue did form, to draw water from the only water point for 16,000 men and it took 4 hours for me to reach it with a dixie. And the queue remained a queue with no distinguishing feature from the crowd engulfing it except the water utensil held in hand.

By the 2nd day, two more water points had been worked into the distribution. We now had two basic necessities – and we also had food.

Our own rationing bodies – having foreseen the possibility of hard times, had been withholding part of our rice issued by the Japanese in the past – saving indeed for this – our rainy day.

Barracks doors provided fuel, water was available, dixies we had brought, rice was held by each 'units' quartermaster, and in that multitude, each 'unit' found it's own dixie of cooked rice from which to draw an equally shared ration.

But with food being prepared and eaten to competition from hundreds of flies which zig zag from the open latrines to our rice dixies, it is very evident that dysentery will sweep us all. In the tropics under these conditions, we had learnt to regard the fly, as a sure killer. At Birdwood camp, we used to net millions in a mosquito bed net as they swarmed up on removing the borehole latrine lid. Yes, a fly could kill and too many were buzzing around for safety

The 2nd night found me working out two digging spells on the latrines, and six spells on using them!

The weakest point in our armour was our bowels.

Cases of diphtheria were being diagnosed by a MO.

An Aussie Chaplain, like a bookie at a crowded race meeting, had fixed up 2 black boards. But this 'honest Joe' was giving us better odds than a gentleman of the turf.

On one board he had written the words of a hymn and on the other, he had chalked out the words of Psalm 23. "The Lord is my Shepherd, I shall not want".

4 RAMC men, who had been caught outside their camp wire some days ago, had been executed so it seemed 'pressure was being applied'.

Lids were made for all the latrine trenches by the fourth day to minimise the fly menace, and everybody enjoyed the pleasure of a heavy downpour of rain. Nature's shower bath was a facility we all used and enjoyed.

By now, the multitude had organised itself into various queues for all purposes – food, water, natural functions.

And each night, two Australian trumpeters softened the low road of hundreds of mens' voices when they rendered in perfect harmony, the Army call of 'Last Post'.

That call seemed like a morale 'jab' reminding us of a more

civilised and ordered way of life – something to hang on for.

I've often wondered if these two went north on the Siam Railway of Death and if they came through OK.

Threats were made on the fourth day to bring in the 'Hospital' – the block at Roberts Barracks housing War wounded and sick cases.

But before that took place, the OC of British and Australian Troops issued an Order. He had a most unenviable task.

"During this period", he said, "the conditions in which you have been placed, have been under my constant consideration. These may be briefly described as such, that existence therein will result in a very few days in the outbreak of epidemic, and the most serious consequences to those under my command and inevitable death to many. Taking into account the low state of health in which many of us now are, and the need to preserve our force intact as long as possible, and in the full conviction that my action, were the circumstances in which we are now living known to them, would meet with the approval of HM Government, I have felt it my duty to order all personnel to sign the Certificate under the duress imposed by the Imperial Japanese Army.

I am fully convinced that HM Government only expect Prisoners of War not to give their parole when such parole is to be given voluntarily. This factor can in no circumstances be regarded as applicable to our present position. The responsibility for this proceeding rests with me and I fully accept it in ordering you to sign. I wish to record in this Order, my deep appreciation of the excellent spirit and good discipline which all ranks have shown during this trying period. I look to all ranks to continue in good heart, discipline and morale.

Thank you for your loyalty and co-operation. Signed Officer Commanding British & Australian Troops. 4th September 1942. Changi".

Later, the camps were dispersed to Thailand and East Asia, many tales of which have already been published.

(End of the Selerang Incident additional notes written by dad after the War).

2 September 1942 : Nippon acts quickly. On morning roll call, we are told to pack our kit by noon. All prisoners are to be confined to Selerang barracks, and to be moved in by 6.30pm. What a day piling cookhouse boilers, rations, kit and equipment onto our engineless motor lorries. Selerang barracks are in the Aussie lines, fortunately hardly a mile for us to push our trucks. The road leading into the lines is soon choc-a-bloc with motor chassis piled perilously high with kit and essentials being pulled, pushed, coaxed and cussed up the hill, while the endless straggling army from the 18th Division, overtaking the slower moving vehicles are hanging as much kit from themselves as ever a human frame was meant to carry. The 18th Division unlike us, have a 2 mile journey from their camp and what they can't carry must be left behind. What we cannot pile onto our trailers, we have time to go back before 6.30pm. Our dinner, previously cooked, is taken over to Selerang in containers, but hardly have we dumped our kit and filed onto the road for our dinner, when the Sikh and Jap sentries come along striking all and sundry. It's their way of telling us to move in onto the barrack square and take the cookhouse with us. Gradually we recognise the new conditions to be imposed on us – and what conditions for an army even a beaten one. Selerang barracks has 7 blocks – the normal peacetime barracks for one battalion of the Gordon Highlanders. Into this is being concentrated the 11th Division, 18th Division, Southern Command, Malayan Command and the Australian Forces. In round figures 16,000 men are being housed in barracks meant for 800 men. The quick nightfall hides the masses on the square. Already squads are detailed and are hacking through the asphalt parade ground to start digging latrines. One of the first things we discovered is that the barracks have had no lavatories since they were put out of order in February, and 16,000 men must have a place to excrete. I pass a restless night on the crowded floor unable to stretch my legs without kicking somebody's back and unable to turn without coming face to face with somebody's feet. I often wake and hear the sentries from outside, changing guard, and from the inside, the grating of picks and shovels as the latrine squads dig down on the barrack square.

3 September 1942 : I can now take in the position as I see it from the roof of the barracks. The barrack buildings from a square, an outer road running round the block. This road is posted with Jap and Sikh sentries armed with bayoneted rifles. A brengun post commands one road and a 2nd machine gun post is being dug by the black triangle men (Jap Military Police). The barrack blocks have 3 floors each. Each block having bedspace for 132 men, but each block is expected to hold 2,000 men. Obviously the barracks are crammed to saturation and still they cannot absorb all the men. Fortunately the roofs of the barracks are flat and these too can be utilised. Tarpaulin tents and bivouacs on the roofs afford shelter for a further couple of hundred. The moving throng on the square at first reminds me of the

London Zoo on a Bank Holiday Monday. But Bank Holiday crowds can escape the pushing and shoving at the end of the day in the privacy of their homes. Looking longer, I can realise our position. In the centre of the barrack square, so that no particular block will get the lion's share of the odour, squads are digging latrine trenches 30 feet long and 18 feet deep. The first trench was wanted so urgently that it only was 10 feet deep before being thrown open to use. 40 such trenches are needed, and these, in 4 rows of 10 with the piles of upturned clay and sand dominate the scene. In the same barrack square within a stones throw of the open latrines, are the cookhouses, numbering about 25 cooking the rice for the men. The death rate among PoWs just after capitulation for dysentery alone, was 300 men a month. Now after 6 months of 90% rice diet, we are all considerably less resistant to disease and with the sun baking the square and breeding flies in the latrines, dysentery is bound to strike down the camp. Even sick cases are not allowed to leave the barracks for hospital and last night, a MO operated successfully for appendicitis. With the cookhouses and latrines taking up a lot of the square, the remainder is soaked up by the overflow of troops who for the want of better accommodation, have pitched their blankets on the barrack square. Through this flood of humanity winds a queue. That is the water queue – I spent 4 hours waiting in it today with a cookhouse dixie. Besides having no sanitation, the barracks had no water laid on. There is a well in the corner of the square from which is drawn the water for the cooking for 16,000 men. Water for washing is so far out of the question. An Aussie Chaplain has put up two black boards, on which he has chalked up Psalm 23 "The Lord is my Shepherd" and a hymn. The whole thing reminds me of the rescue camps one might see after a national disaster such as an earthquake. Our Colonel tonight tells us how Colonel

Holmes, our CC, has explained to the Japs that these conditions will result in the inevitable death of many. The first morning's sick parade alone has shown 3 cases of diphtheria, and 50 cases of dysentery already in the camp. The 4 RAMS men caught some days ago outside their wire have been shot so the Japs mean business. Rather than let disease kill off so many, Colonel Holmes has warned us he may issue an Order ordering every man to sign the parole form. I pass a very unsettled night between working 2 night spells on the digging and also by a spell of dysentery. I came in with loose bowels so I hope that I can get them righted again before they start trouble.

4 September 1942 : Yesterday, was normally ration day but no rations have arrived. With no rations or fuel for the cookhouse fires they have us beaten. But so far, the food situation is OK for most Regimental Mess Officers have long foreseen such a time as this, and have built up a reserve from the rations in the past. The rice with powdered soup from the recent Red Cross ship keeps our bellies full. Doors are being used for firewood, whilst other wood is being made into trapdoors to cover the latrines and minimise the fly menace. Two other water points have been tapped into a water main by the REs, so with 3 water points, the water situation is eased. We can even manage a wash – 20 men to a bucket and the last man performing his ablutions in a couple of inches of soap lather and sediment. Everyone queues, for food, water, even for physical needs. The afternoon brings a heavy downpour and many take this opportunity of using natures shower baths. Tonight at roll call, we are told in our own interests that we must sign.........

"Accordingly I, the undersigned, do most solemnly swear

that I will not attempt escape. W Holt. Gunner. British (English). Changi. 5/9/42".

5 September 1942 : This morning, I reported at the Australian MO and got some binding mixture for my inside. We are now told we can move back to our own camps so once more our trailers are packed high with kit and pulled to our old areas. It is so nice to be back once more in our comfortable camp that it makes me wonder how good it will feel like to be home. The Japs, as if to atone for their 'severity measures' have issued us our rations on a bigger scale than we normally have.

8 October 1942 : I once read it is possible to live on four foods. A) Wholemeal bread, B) Milk, C) Green Vegetables, D) Potatoes. These four foods supply all the vitamins necessary for the body's needs. Yet consider our diet as compared to this. We eat Rice. Rice contains starch so that clears the fourth food potatoes (also starch). But bread we do not have, milk is equally impossible but we do get a 2oz issue of vegetables per man which when boiled, comes down to one dessert spoonful. Rice takes 1 hour to digest, European food about 4 or 5 hours. Rice may be nutritious back home but rice back home is made with eggs and milk – not boiled in water. The Japs know the diet is sadly lacking so they give us Amenity pay – as a gunner I get 10 cents a day with which to buy extra food, but Canteen prices are high. Fortunately as a non-smoker I spend all my money on food and not tempted to buy the abominable Chinese cigarettes to satisfy a smoker's craving. For 10 cents I can buy nearly ½ lb of peanuts which contain Vitamin B which I know is so vital for our health. By saving 10 days pay I can buy 6 eggs and by saving 5 days pay I can buy a pint of palm oil for it's vitamins. 21 days pay will buy a pound of margarine for it's vitamins A and D. I have a tin now, it isn't always available. It is French stuff from Indo China presumably. Thus by spending wisely I hope I can keep reasonably healthy. The hospital already is crowded with Beri Beri cases – and this only after a few months of this food.

Beri Beri is paralysis caused through a lack of vitamin B. Even in the Regiment now, very many men - not bad enough for the hospital - but suffering from cracked mouths, their feet and bones so painful that sleep is practically impossible, slight dropsy in the legs – all caused through the deficiencies in the diet. The MOs know only European food can prevent this. Here is an example on the one vitamin B which rice contains. 3,000 units of vitamin B are necessary daily but an Army estimate says 1,600 units of vitamin B is the minimum for health. To get the minimum vitamin B from rice I would have to eat 4lbs daily. But as a man's ration is 1lb, I am only getting half of the necessary units vitamin B a day. I had started buying rice polishings to make up the deficiency for the polishings although they taste like sawdust, are said to contain the nourishment of the rice. Then there are fats, and other foods which we must have for vitamins A, B, D and so on. I believe the Div Sigs buy sharks oil for the vitamin A. But while I am saving up for one food for it's vitamins it is always at the expense of some other foods I could buy for other vitamins equally necessary – it seems a losing race to prevent these horrible complaints which even include blindness. If I can keep healthy until my relief, I will have really achieved something. It seems more dangerous to be a PoW than to fight among shot, shells, and bombs.

14 October 1942 : I am feeling on top of the shop tonight – thanks to the Red Cross. If only an International body could settle national differences in the same way in which this organisation can relieve distress irrespective of nationality or race. Cocoa, biscuits, sugar, milk, jam, tinned meat and veg – enough foodstuffs have been sent from South Africa and India to make the rice diet enjoyable over a period of weeks if used properly. Thanks South Africa. They gave us a swell time in our weeks stay at Cape Town and even now as prisoners, they have not forgotten us. There are 65 cigarettes per man too, from India. Everyone is smoking strong, the air is thick like wet burning straw. As usual, when spirits are high, the war rumours (PARAGRAPH CUT OUT FROM DIARY).

It has cropped up in various times in different stories since then; and now everyone is happy, it's about time it came up again. Tonight we are getting a cup of cocoa and biscuits, we are getting beans for tomorrow's breakfast, fruit after dinner and bully stew. It's quite a pleasure, this PoW life.

Chapter Seventeen

IN CHINA SEAS

25 October – 14 November 1942

A 1,000 of us, together with 1,000 Nip troops are abroad the 'England Maru' bound for Japan. I am sorry to leave Singapore. We are crowded in the holds of the ship, I being in the forward hold. The open hatches, thank God, do let in a little ventilation for with 250 in this forward hold with no man with sleeping space enough to stretch, the heat is terrific. We are allowed up on deck for 2 to 3 hours a day. Fresh water is limited – in fact almost unobtainable and as usual, when anything is unavailable, I want it all the more. During the night we ran through a hailstorm. As sleep was now impossible with the stuffiness and with the rain and waves pouring into the hold flooding our sleeping quarters, I went up on deck and had a glorious bath in the hail and drank my fill of water from a deck house rain gutter. On 11 November we had a short Armistice service down in the hold, although the Padre wasn't allowed to have hymns sung. The solemn note of the service was destroyed by 2 large waves which hit the bows and cascaded in a waterfall down the open hold and over the Padre. (PARAGRAPH CUT FROM DIARY).

Singapore 1942 (Taken from an additional notebook written by dad after the War)

Three weeks in the hold of the "England Maru" had not given us the benefits one might expect from an Oriental cruise. Our 'old man' did protest on our behalf, and the Nips beat him all over the deck for his trouble.

We weren't wanted on voyage.
We were stowed accordingly.
We were wanted in Formosa.

Once disembarked, they drove us to the Mountains. Not by trucks. Trucks don't grow on trees. Bamboo does. So they drove us with bamboo sticks.

Little villages, through which we passed, turned out hundreds of blank faced villagers. No hostility was shown. Formosans didn't exactly love the Japs either.

The camp 'buncho' gave his welcoming speech. "You should have hung at Singapore" he said. Pause for translation which robbed the statement of it's punch.

"You may redeem your honour and work diligently in Mine. If you work, you eat". A simple enough code. I started copper mining on Christmas Day. My number was "Ni Yong Yong". We "bangoed" off in Nipponese, then climbed down the mountain as if to the sea. It was a lovely rugged holiday postcard view. It made you want to post a card off to Mum.

Mum got her first card 2 years later – my card was a workers privilege.

"They" worded it for me. They ended my card with the Legend "Look after my life and welfare". I signed this – block letters.

I've wondered what we meant by that on our card – Nip and I.

"Hatsmo" – we doffed miners hats and bowed low to the Spirits at the Pithead Shrine.

To my own God I prayed for safety.

"Kapsmo" – hats on, lamps lit and we filed into the Mountain and into the mine.

"Hi-ho Hi-ho, it's off to work we go". Whistling, like the seven little dwarfs, I was off to my work in a mine.

That's how I earned my first clout. Snow White – tell your charges that whistling in mines causes roof falls.

We hopped from sleeper to sleeper along the main drag, dodging the loaded body trains. Two miles before we reached the Cages. Into a cage – it dropped into the earth like a hawk from it's sky. Hundreds of feet and stopped two seconds ahead of our stomachs.

"Ticker" was my mine Hancho.
He sadly resembled a Hippo. He bellowed and shouted – but seldom struck out.
Not like, for example, the "Ghost".
He wandered the workings in darkness,
Spying for "non-diligent workers being betrayed by the light of their lamps.
He chastised with his hammer.

We worked without supervision. Production was assessed at say, 6 bogies per man.

Two men in a hole meant 12 bogies of Kosaki to be mined for Tojo.

While one man pushed full bogies down to the cage returning with an empty, his mate filled the spare at the chute.

Tracks sloped towards the cage.

Your loaded bogy, once started, needed little effort on it's half mile run.

Many rode the buffers along the completely black tunnels. You crouched low, of course to avoid scraping your back on the air pipes slung from the low roof.

You clanged this pipe with a stone, warning up traffic bogies to find a siding. The clangs travelled far.

Tools were limited to chunkal and basket.

Men were expendable – tools were not.

Lose a tool – gain a hiding.

Understand, therefore, the concern of these two chaps. They had jumped clear when half a ton of glistening Kosaki had dropped from the roof. And there was the chunkal handle sticking out from under that slab. They couldn't lift to free that chunkal head no how.

Neither could 2 Chinese drillers who had entered the hole. They didn't try.

They simply excavated a little hole in the ground beneath the trapped chunkal head – which obligingly dropped through.

Damned clever these Chinese.

Dunky and I weren't cut out for manual work not even under duress. (Easier stopped than started).

Pack the bogy with this old timber, top up with a dressing of Kosaki and there you have a nice quick bogy load.

"Ni Yong Yong" I shouted to the Chinese checker boy, as I slewed the fast moving bogy past his checkpoint. From here, the run was lighted right down to the cage.

But the top heavy bogy jumped the points. The strewn timber shouted "See this". And grateful was I for a good conditioned hat which took most of Hancho's hammer blow.

That's how I qualified for Naisaki jobs. Some holes had barely 2 feet ceiling room. Also 'hotspots' where you worked in 30 second spurts. The heat and hot rain falling from the roof drove you out of the hole for gasps. When the air was foul, you coiled a wire round the flame jet to keep your lamp burning. The red hot wire re-ignites the acetylene gas as soon as you reach air which allows combustion.

Despite the prayers at the Pithead shrine, our safety lay in Other Hands.

For every mine fatality or accident there were 50 miracle misses. There was the roof fall along the 20 yard gap between 2 squads filing along to the cage.

With production low, the Japs originated the Do-it-Yourself movement.

On return to Camp, the non-diligent squads had to "turn and face your partner". Then proceed to hit one another for all your worth.

Rifle butts helped the hesitant.

Stunt men could have learnt much from pulled punches and grunts, that day.

After the stick – the carrot.

> "An extra rice ball for extra production".
> "Grub up".
> "This bucket for extra rice balls".
> "You Jap happy bathbuns".
> "I say it's better to work for rice than be sick without".
> "That extra bogy takes more than a rice ball gives".
> "They can stick their rice balls – I'm not doing more".
> "They wont carry me up Boot Hill".

Nearly 400 came to the Camp. Already 100 lie buried at Boot Hill.

Boot Hill was laid out in terraces on the hillside, each terrace was wide as a coffin is long. Ronald laid down to judge the width before cutting the next terrace. OMENS? Ronald was trying for size. He made a good fit.......3 weeks later.

20 working men in a 20 man Squad meant 20 bowls of rice in a bucket.
Sick men's ration was ¼ of a bowl from the bucket.
"14 rations this morning lads - 9 men are sick".
"Alright lads, share alike". ¼ of a bowl each. Half the Squad is sick".
"Let's share alike lads".
"Not me, I'm not going down on half a bowl, I need my ration for 6 bogies".
"You can't give a sick man a bowl".
"A worker is entitled to his ration".
"They're sick".
"We're ALL sick".
Yet sick men had friends – especially if they couldn't face their ration.
No fun being BIOKI in camp....Life was made unpleasant.
3 "dysentery's" caught playing cards were manacled together 21 days. (Once to the benjo for yourself – twice for your friends).
The fear of the mine kept some "sick" as long as possible – even on starvation rations. Food was the sole conversational topic. Recipes were written and read. The pass for work to the mine for "dysentery's" was a solid 'specimen'. So for this daily inspection, many a sick man 'survived' by borrowing from an ailing friend when their 'own' was no longer reliable.
The Camp strength grew to 600. Newly arrived and suntanned, the fresh draft looked aghast at the returning miners – grey skinned, brown stained and skinny.
"You've lost morale" they said.
"You've let it get you".
"It can't be that bad" they hoped.
Well, later it wasn't. Things improved.

The midnight and 3am roll calls ceased. We had a 'rest day' every 3 weeks, on which a church service was allowed. We nearly lost it through "Onward Christian Soldiers". We nearly had prayer books till "they" saw the dedication "To The Time The Rising Sun Sets and the Crooked Cross Unfolds".

No more did we bow to the East at Reveille shouting Sai Kerri in salute to the Emperor. Those nearest the doors still got Rifle butts on reveille, and a Rubber neck, the 2nd in command, who had a twitch and a mouthful of front teeth, still threw his bucket of water over the last man out.
Then came Red Cross (4 parcels in 3½ years). Thanks indeed, even for the tins of creamed RICE! The bulk medical supplies for Malaria might have been appreciated – but we were above the Malaria belt. No doubt our Mine dressings went to a jungle camp.

Then credit accounts for workers! 1 month in the mine could earn enough credit for a bottle of Wakomoto Vitamin B Tablets. "For Beri Beri" said the label in English – "Improves the Appetite" !!
We learnt diet deficiencies cause ailments.
No B1 causes Beri Beri.
No salt causes Cramp.
No fat causes skin to crack.
The itching, we discover, was caused by Lice. By wearing your shirt inside out every other day, you keep them on the move. This gives temporary relief.

Remember Jock's "Changi Beri" in the early days in Changi. The MO still had some Western foods left then. "Take this Marmite" he said, "it contains Vitamin B". Jock smeared this valuable food like an ointment all over his unmentionable.

We've come a long way since then. So had the Yanks who were flying around these days.
The siren for the village – it's wooden shacks stacked up the mountain opposite, had broken down.
Three voices rendered a 'wailing winnie' over the public amplifier speaker – the perfect harmony trio. Then to the thud of distant bombs, they boosted civilian morale by playing the rousing march 'Blaze Away'.
We didn't like the look of the tunnel being dug from the camp into the mine.
"Shelters" said the Guards.
"More likely to do us in" we said, "As soon as the Yanks invade".

But the Yanks passed by onto Okinowa. But the Senior PoW in the camp did know of their plan to exterminate us in the tunnel and had already selected 5 of the healthiest to break away in the hopes that one could reach the coast with the story.
Newspapers were smuggled in from the mine. A Sgt had learnt hundreds of Chinese characters to decipher this news. News was filtered to us gradually for security – it was good.

Bob foolishly entered on 'rumour' in his diary. It was picked up by the only English-speaking Goon. It cost Bob a nasty beating and a broken jaw. It was broken again later when it healed.

The Island was always now on 'Alert'.
"We'll see McArthur coming over the hill yet" we said.
Then suddenly, off we were sent to the jungle.
A camp to make from scratch.
Trees to fell. Roof to thatch.
"Speedo" from dawn to dusk.

Nakajima was driving his Guards and their captives relentlessly.
He knocked two men senseless daily. Joe Polack, the Polish American, had been tied standing in the sun for many days, fed daily on 2 rice balls and salt.
Smithers and Flint had gone 'nuts'.

Everybodys' noses stuck out more, eyes went further back.

Then it was over.

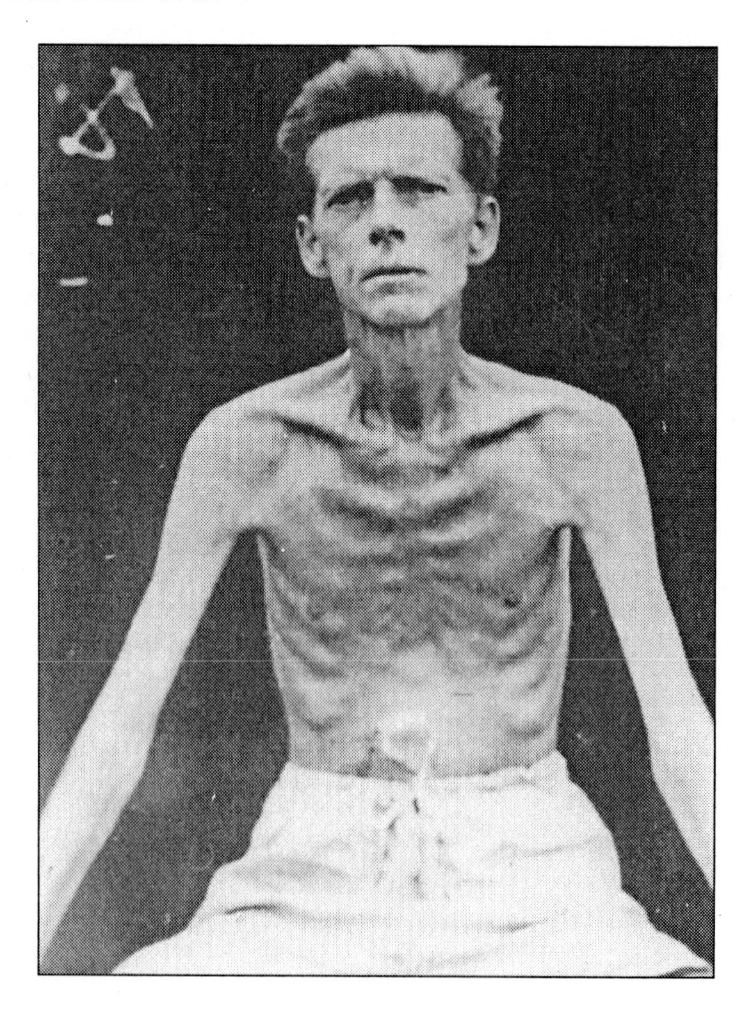

Had been for some days!

Guards vanished overnight.

Red Cross relief from the air. The heavy bales failed to open the chutes. Some crashed through the huts killing and maiming. Fancy praying for bully beef then it killing you.

We tore the chutes into ground strips spelling "STOP".

And the big American Marines came, cleaned us, fattened us, and let us see the Hula girls in Hawaii on our way across the Pacific.

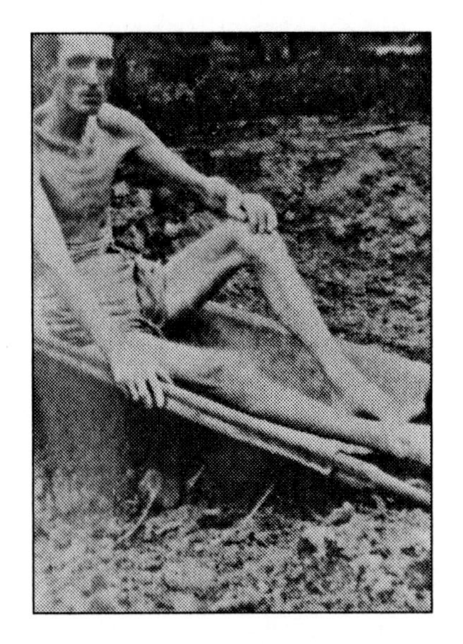

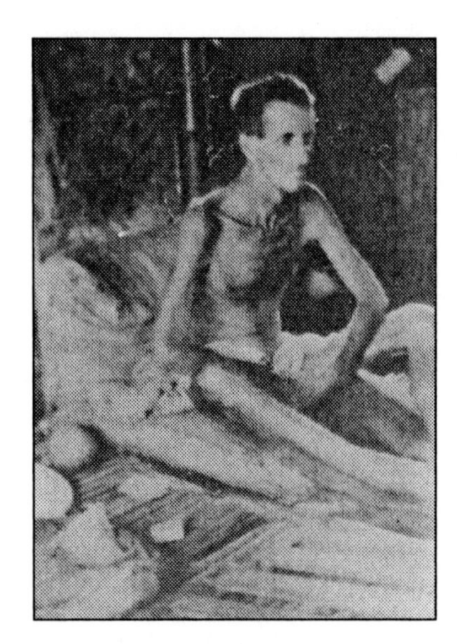

(End of the notes taken from an additional notebook written by dad after the War).

The Jap troops are trading cigarettes for our pullovers. If they want pullovers, it must be a cold place we are bound for so I will hang on to mine. Food is quite good, rice and a tasty vegetable gypo 3 times a day. My main complaint is these crowded quarters, diarrhoea and these damned cursed China Seas. My Stomach ! (AT THIS POINT THREE PAGES HAVE BEEN CUT FROM THE DIARY).

Something Funny :

We filed into the prisoner's office for interrogation. At the table sat the Nipponese Officer with pen, ink and forms. At his side sat 'Pop', our interpreter. 'Pop' learnt his English through his civilian employment in the American branch of a Nipponese firm, he wasn't too hot on the interpretation side of his job either. Each man, he asked in turn, the question "What was your civilian trade?". Answers such as 'clerk', 'baker', etc, he could translate to the officer straight away. But some answers such a 'welder' or 'labourer' had to be more fully explained before he could translate the Nipponese equivalent.

It came to Fred Holmes' turn for questioning. Fred is a foreman navvy.

Pop – "What was your civilian trade?"
Fred – "I was a ganger, Sir."
Pop jerked back six inches in his chair, his mouth slightly opened in astonishment. He turned as if to translate the reply to the officer at his side, but thought it better to make sure of things first. He looked Fred squarely in the eye and leaning forward again, said "You are sure of that? You are a gangster?"

December 1943 : Taiwan
After 2 years feeding on rice for 3 meals every day, here is how a fellow PoW expresses himself, in verse :

Rice !!

There's an article of diet
That's enough to cause a riot
You'll agree if you just try it.
It is Rice.

It's the regular daily winner
Breakfast, supper, tea or dinner
It would make a saint a sinner
All this Rice.

You can boil it, you can bake it
You can grind it, mould it, cake it
But no matter how you fake it
Still it's Rice.

You can fry it up with gammon
You can mix up with tin salmon
Even lots of strawberry jam on
Won't change Rice.

When you wake up in the morning
You won't do the usual yawning
You'll just run without a warning
Oh! this Rice.

Even if you are quite diabetic
It will make you very athletic
It's the perfect diuretic
It's the Rice.

Ladies, when this war is over
Bells will ring from York to Dover
If you want to be in clover
Don't say Rice.

All your days can be quite palmy
When your man comes home from the Army
But three words will send him barmy
"Have some Rice".

Whilst on the subject of verse, I would like to add this 12 line sonnet on the battle, the result of which landed us here as PoWs, 12,000 miles from home :

Fortress of Singapore

A mighty Island Fortress
The guardian of the East
An up to date Gibraltar
A thousand planes at least.

It simply can't be taken
We'll stand a siege for years
We'll hold this place for ever
Twill bring our foes to tears.

Our men are here in thousands
Defences are unique
The Japs did not believe it
So they took it in a week!

Chapter Eighteen

SETTING OF THE RISING SUN

December 1943

Another Xmas abroad. Each time, yuletide comes, I say I hope my next is at home. I have promised myself an Xmas at home, when I arrive there, no matter at what time of year it may be.

My Xmases Abroad

Xmas nineteen thirty nine
I spent at Auchy, Northern France
Waiting for a Nazi sign
That he was starting an advance.

Old fashioned Xmas. Biting cold
Broad fields a sea of shimmering white
Our gunpits ready, netting rolled
Alert "stood to", prepared to fight.

Yet in this season, was this not when
Should be Earth Peace, Goodwill toward men?

Following Xmas, one nine four owe
In 'Bonnie Scotland', bleak and drear
There, yuletide takes a second place
To next week's festival – New Year.

Drab Xmas this, no joy bells rang
In this quiet sleepy Lothian town
A canteen helped me quell the pang
Of loneliness, and meanwhile down.

In war torn London, mother, dad
And all at home made their brave show
Despite the bombing, to be glad
And festive in a world of woe.

Xmas time, yet, this is when
Should be Earth Peace, Goodwill to all men?

Xmas, nineteen forty one
Malayan jungles. Tropic hell
We sent our yuletide messages
To Nip troops with each four five shell.

Our Xmas joint was bully beef
I washed mine down with luke warm tea
Our Xmas gifts? Planes, spreading death
Life was precious, death too free.

Such madness loosed abroad and when
Should be Earth Peace, Goodwill to all men?

Xmas, nineteen forty two
I'm down a mine. Prisoner of War
Sweating, toiling in the Earth's deep bowels
Compelled to mine for copper ore.

My Xmas lunch, a box of rice
I ate whilst sitting on a stone
When would peace come, and at what price?
Would I spend next year's yuletide at home?

Would next year be an Xmas when
There really would be peace to all men?
Next year is now, still Prisoner of War
But I've every hope pinned on 1944.

(DIARY CONFISCATED DECEMBER 1943).

On return of the diary and written in pencil on the last two blank pages, (the very last 6 pages having been ripped from the covers), there is a record my dad – Bill Holt kept of his weight as a PoW, waiting for freedom:

1942

Oct	10st 6 lbs
Dec	10st 4 lbs

1943

Jan	8st 13lbs
Mar	8st 0lbs
May	9st 4lbs
Jul	9st 0 lbs
Sep	8st 10lbs
Oct	9st 1lbs
Nov	8st 6lbs

1944

Jan	9st 4lbs
Feb	9st 4lbs
Mar	9st 6 lbs
Apr	9st 9½ lbs

May	9st 9½ lbs	
Jun	10st 5lbs	
Jul	10st 6lbs	
Aug	10st 1lbs	
Sep	10st 4lbs	
Oct	10st 1lbs	
Nov	9st 13lbs	
Dec	9st 13lbs	
1945		
Jan	9st 13lbs	
Feb	9st 11lbs	
Mar	9st 10lbs	
Apr	9st 7lbs	
May	9st 1½ lbs	
Jun	8st 12lbs	
Jul	8st 6lbs	
Aug	Freedom any day.	
Sep	5th	8st 2lbs
	13th	9st 8lbs
	18th	10st 2lbs
Oct	14th	11st 9lbs.

* * * * *

BUCKINGHAM PALACE

The Queen and I bid you a very warm welcome home.

Through all the great trials and sufferings which you have undergone at the hands of the Japanese, you and your comrades have been constantly in our thoughts. We know from the accounts we have already received how heavy those sufferings have been. We know also that these have been endured by you with the highest courage.

We mourn with you the deaths of so many of your gallant comrades.

With all our hearts, we hope that your return from captivity will bring you and your families a full measure of happiness, which you may long enjoy together.

George R.I.

September 1945.

The author of 'Bamboo & Bushido', Alf Allbury, who was the sole survivor of a Japanese PoW ship which was torpedoed, and who was rescued after a week clinging to a raft, got to know my dad after the war when they both worked in London for the General Post Office. Over a cup of tea they got talking about their war experiences and it was dad who persuaded and helped Alf to write his book. On the inside cover of 'Bamboo & Bushido' Alf wrote "To Bill Holt, he probably had a lousier time than I did – but he wouldn't talk about it like I have. Best wishes, Alf Allbury". How very true are those words, now having read dad's personal account.

I was 39 when dad died, but I never heard dad talk about his war experiences or saw him sit comfortably watching Japanese war films. Having only now read his diary for the very first time (while typing it initially for mum), I still feel that he had not fully released his feelings through his diary.

In December 1983, 'Reader's Digest' ran a special feature called 'The Man Sent From God' telling another moving story of quiet heroism in a Japanese PoW camp. On this occasion the diary was kept by a Major Ben Wheeler, a young Canadian Doctor, but like dad, risking severe punishment, they thought it worth the risk.

Printed in the United Kingdom
by Lightning Source UK Ltd.
118154UK00001B/46